Great
Political ☆☆
Wit ☆

P9-DFU-018

BY BOB DOLE

Historical Almanac of the United States Senate

*Trusting the People: The Dole-Kemp Plan to Free
the Economy and Create a Better America*

*Great Political Wit: Laughing (Almost) All the Way
to the White House*

[WITH ELIZABETH DOLE]

Unlimited Partners: Our American Story

Great Political  Wit

LAUGHING *(Almost)* ALL THE WAY
TO THE WHITE HOUSE

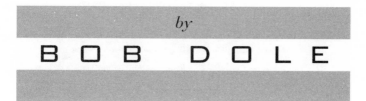

by

BOB DOLE

BROADWAY BOOKS
NEW YORK

A hardcover edition of this book was originally published in 1998 by Doubleday. It is here reprinted by arrangement with Doubleday.

GREAT POLITICAL WIT. copyright © 1998 by Bob Dole.
Afterword copyright © 2000 by Bob Dole. All rights reserved.
Printed in the United States of America.
No part of this book may be reproduced or transmitted
in any form or by any means, electronic or mechanical, including
photocopying, recording, or by any information storage and retrieval system,
without written permission from the publisher.
For information, address: Broadway Books,
a division of Random House, Inc.,
1540 Broadway, New York, NY 10036.

Broadway Books titles may be purchased for business or promotional use
or for special sales. For information, please write to:
Special Markets Department, Random House, Inc.,
1540 Broadway, New York, NY 10036.

BROADWAY BOOKS and its logo, a letter B bisected on the diagonal,
are trademarks of Broadway Books,
a division of Random House, Inc.

Visit our website at www.broadwaybooks.com

First Broadway Books trade paperback edition published 2000.

Designed by Judith Stagnitto Abbate / Abbate Design

Library of Congress Cataloging-in-Publication Data

Great political wit: laughing (almost) all the way to the White House / Bob Dole—1st Broadway Books trade pbk. ed.
    p. cm.
Originally published: New York: Doubleday, 1998.
ISBN 0-7679-0667-5
    1. United States—Politics and government—20th century—Humor.
2. United States—Politics and government—20th century—Quotations,
maxims, etc.   3. American wit and humor.   4. Politicians—United
States—Quotations.   5. Dole, Robert J., 1923–   I. Dole, Robert J., 1923–
E743.G736 2000
973.929′092—dc21   00-041370

01   02   03   04   10   9   8   7   6   5   4   3

To Elizabeth and Robin,
who have filled my life with laughter

Acknowledgments

———— ☆ ————

THERE ARE MANY DIFFERENCES between Capitol Hill and the private sector, but one thing they have in common is the fact that it is important to surround yourself with good people. Throughout this project, I was fortunate to be able to call upon the assistance of three talented individuals—Richard Norton Smith, Kerry Tymchuk, and Joyce Campbell. Richard, Kerry, and Joyce all worked for me at one time or another in the United States Senate, and I appreciate their continuing loyalty, counsel, and laughter.

A special thanks to Bill Adler, who first proposed the idea of this book, and to Doubleday's Nan A. Talese, who helped turn the proposal into a reality.

Finally, thanks to all those—both in and out of office—who provided the material for this book. Here's hoping that Americans are laughing with us and not at us.

Contents

———— ☆ ————

Foreword	xi
Roots	1
Public Speaking	7
Campaigning	18
Politicians	30
Defeat	46
The Presidency	53
The Vice Presidency	63
The White House	70
All in the Family	75
The Media	87
Governing	99
The Economy	107
Religion	114
War	121
Off Hours	125
Politics as Usual	137
Free Advice	150
Partisanship	160
Liberal/Conservative	174
Retirement	180
Late Night	186
Afterword	191

Foreword

───── ☆ ─────

THE TRADITIONAL FATE of candidates who lose a presidential election is to spend several weeks in seclusion or on vacation, ruminating about what went wrong and what might have yielded a different result at the polls. And I suspect after the votes were counted on November 5, 1996, there were many political observers who thought that I would continue that tradition by flying off with Elizabeth to a sunny location.

To be sure, I hadn't given much thought to what I would be doing in the weeks following the election. Having studied the public opinion polls, I had a strong suspicion that I wouldn't be picking a cabinet, but during a campaign your entire focus is on getting to election day. And so when I delivered my concession speech that evening, I meant it when I said, "Tomorrow is the first day of my life when I have nothing to do."

When I got up the next morning, I discovered that

I was wrong. My first stop was "Dole for President" headquarters in Washington, D.C., where I began the process of personally thanking the hundreds and hundreds of staffers and volunteers who worked for my campaign, and placing calls to hundreds more across the country. What got my attention that day, however, was not a call I placed, but one that came in to my office. It was from the producers of *The Late Show with David Letterman.* They were to be broadcasting from Washington, D.C., in two nights—would I be interested in being a guest?

Two nights later, Dave and I sat onstage, trading quips. Dave asked me about a favorite topic of his— President Clinton's weight. "I don't know," was my comeback. "I never tried to lift him. I just tried to beat him." The audience laughed, and pundits, ever quick to grasp the obvious, claimed to have discovered a New Dole.

I suppose you could say my postpolitical career really began on that Friday night as viewers discovered that I wasn't the glowering, Social Security-devouring sourpuss they'd come to know, if not to like, from watching all those attack ads made possible by White House coffee drinkers.

Within a matter of weeks, I had also appeared on *The Tonight Show with Jay Leno,* taped a cameo on the Brooke Shields situation comedy, *Suddenly Susan,* appeared on *Saturday Night Live,* and filmed a

Visa card commercial—which premiered during the 1997 Super Bowl—in which I returned to my hometown of Russell, Kansas, only to have my local diner's waitress ask me for identification before I could cash a check. "I just can't win," I lamented at the end of the commercial.

By going on television so soon after my defeat to poke fun at the campaign just concluded, I hoped to shatter the tradition of presidential also-ran silence. Most of all, I wanted to show that there is indeed life after politics. And that losing an election does not mean losing your sense of humor.

As with so much in my life, I owe my sense of humor to Russell, Kansas, the community that provides my roots and a constant source of strength. My first job as a teenager was working at Dawson's Drug Store in downtown Russell. For a few dollars a day, I whipped up chocolate malteds behind the soda fountain, and gave curb service on weekends. And I learned from the Dawson brothers that the more you traded quips and one-liners with the customers, the longer they stayed, the more they bought, and the bigger the tips. A few years later, I was to become one of countless veterans who discovered that a sense of humor was essential to surviving surgery, pain, and month upon month of hospitalization. When I returned to Russell to continue my recovery from my war wounds, one of the songs I would play most frequently on the jukebox at Dawson's was "Laughing on the Outside, Crying on the Inside."

Huck Boyd, who was one of my early political mentors, once warned me, "We don't need a Jack Benny in Washington." Actually, the way Uncle Sam spends money, we could use an army of them. I rarely disagreed with Huck, but over the years I've grown ever more convinced that my hero, Dwight Eisenhower, was absolutely right when he said, "A sense of humor is part of the art of leadership, of getting along with people, of getting things done." Indeed, there were countless occasions during my thirty-six years in the halls of Congress—especially the eleven years I served as Senate Republican leader—when a timely one-liner broke the tension at a tough negotiation and got everyone moving toward a solution.

And so I jumped at the opportunity when Doubleday suggested that I put together a few of my favorite stories and political jokes. You may have read or heard some of the stories I have selected. Others may be new to you. All, I hope, will cause you to smile. Even if they confirm your suspicion that politics itself is a joke.

So from crafting legislation, I've gone on to a new career which includes pitching doughnuts. Thus it seems only appropriate that I conclude with a doughnut story. Early in the Clinton administration, I attended yet another in a seemingly endless string of early morning White House meetings. As I left the Oval Office following the meeting, one member of the press corps shouted out how I thought the meeting went. "O.K.," was my response, and then I added, "but it would have been better had they served some doughnuts."

The press corps laughed, and reported my comments. A few days later, I received a letter from a woman in New Jersey who was taken aback at my remark, and thought it showed a lack of seriousness toward the problems facing our country. I wrote back to the woman, explaining that it would be tough to survive in Washington, D.C., without a sense of humor, and that government would be for the worse if public servants were denied the opportunity to laugh at themselves and each other. I hope this book also makes that point. By the way, the next early morning White House meeting I attended following my remark was highlighted by a big plate of doughnuts displayed prominently on the cabinet table. No joke.

Great
Political ☆ ☆
Wit

Roots

———— ☆ ————

THE LATE JOHN CONNALLY liked to tell a story about his Texas roots. In boasting of his background, Big John included George Washington in the Lone Star State's pantheon of heroes. As he told the story, young George one day went out into the backyard with a hatchet in hand and chopped down the family's mesquite tree. In due course he was summoned inside by a very angry parent.

"Did you chop down my mesquite tree?" demanded George's father.

"I cannot tell a lie, Father," said George. "I did chop down your mesquite tree."

On hearing this, the elder Washington ordered his son to start packing his bags. "We're moving to Virginia," he announced.

"Why, Father? Is it because I chopped down your mesquite tree?"

"No, George," came the reply. "Because if you

can't tell a lie, you'll never amount to anything in Texas."

One of President Lyndon Johnson's favorite stories concerned another Texas stem-winder—Senator Tom Connolly—who liked nothing better than to regale listeners with unending descriptions of the state's scenic wonders. Connolly started off in the beautiful piney woods of East Texas. Then he moved on rhetorically through the bluebonnets and out to the plains and down through the Hill Country to the Gulf Coast. Eventually he got back to the piney woods—and started all over again.

The senator had just completed a second tour of the state, and was about to make yet another circuit of gorgeous woods and bluebonnets, when an elderly man rose in the back of the room and yelled out, "The next time you pass Lubbock how about letting me off?"

Though lacking in mesquite trees or piney woods, Kansas has plenty of untamed nature. Tornadoes. Blizzards. Crop failures. When I was growing up there were dust storms as terrifying as the swarms of grasshoppers reported by earlier generations. Airborne armies of them were so immense that they blotted out the sun. It was said, with a gift for exaggeration that would do a Texan proud, that the hoppers were so big they ate the noses of pigs. As for the prairie wind, Kansans like to say that if it steals your hat, you needn't bother running after it; the next gust is sure to bring a replacement.

People who laugh at the elements aren't likely to take politicians very seriously—especially politicians who take themselves that way. Irreverence is in my blood. As I wrote in the Foreword, I owe my sense of humor to Russell, the small Kansas town with the big heart that has always been a source of strength. My father—"Doley" to his friends—ran a cream and egg business, supplementing his income during Prohibition by selling a little bootleg whiskey on the side. Most of his customers gathered at the creamery station, however, not to quench their thirst, but to indulge their need to laugh.

☆ ☆ ☆

"A man's rootage is more important than his leafage."

—WOODROW WILSON

☆

Calvin Coolidge was once asked, "Mr. President, do the people where you come from say 'A hen lays' or 'A hen lies'?"

Coolidge replied, "The people where I come from, sir, lift her up to see."

At a White House reception, a guest approached Coolidge and said, "Mr. President, I'm from Boston!"
Coolidge replied, "You'll never get over it."

☆

Harry Truman was known all his life for his plain speaking. When he made a speech at the Washington Garden Club, he kept referring to the "good manure" that needed to be used on the flowers. Some society women complained to his wife, Bess. "Couldn't you get the President to say 'fertilizer'?" they asked. Mrs. Truman replied, "Heavens no. It took me twenty-five years to get him to say 'manure.'"

☆

On one occasion, Barry Goldwater—whose family owned a department store in Phoenix—found himself wearing a tuxedo with watered-silk lapels in a rather tasteless flowery pattern. "One thing about owning a store," he explained, "you've got to wear the things that don't sell."

Goldwater the Arizonian once expressed his envy of the state of Minnesota with its many inland lakes and waterways: "Out where I come from, we have so little water that the trees chase the dogs."

★

Representative Thomas "Tip" O'Neill of Massachusetts often told a Kennedy family joke, one that JFK particularly enjoyed. In this yarn, the youngest member of the clan, Edward Kennedy, appears in a probate court to have his name changed.

"One of my brothers is President," the senator tells the judge, "and another is Attorney General. I want to make it on my own. I don't want to have a name like Kennedy that is so well known politically."

"I can understand that," the judge says. "What name do you want instead of Teddy Kennedy?"

"I'd like to keep Teddy," he replied, "and change my last name to Roosevelt."

☆

Former Arizona congressman Mo Udall grew up in St. Johns, Arizona (which then had a population of 1,400), a town so small that the entering and leaving signs were hung from the same post. He was fond of joking, "A friend was nine years old before he found out that our town was not named Resume Speed."

Public Speaking

―――――― ☆ ――――――

ANYTHING THAT KEEPS a politician humble is good for democracy. Back in 1961, when I was a young congressman visiting Indiana on the mashed potato circuit, the name Bob Dole had little marquee value. So the local dinner chairman resorted to drastic measures in hopes of hyping the box office. On arriving in town, I was whisked off to the local radio station, where the announcer gave a more or less accurate rendition of my résumé.

"The guest at this evening's dinner," he began, "will be Congressman Bob Doyle [sic]. He will speak at the American Legion Hall. Tickets have been slashed from three dollars to one dollar. A color television set will be given away. You must be present to win, and we're not going to draw until Congressman Doyle gets through talking. Doyle was born in Kansas, raised in Kansas, educated at the University of Kansas. Prior to World War II he was a premedical student. He fought in Italy, where he suffered a serious head injury. Then he went into politics."

By the time I was nominated for Vice President in Kansas City in 1976, most people managed to at least spell my name right. Just in case I was in any danger of getting a swelled head, I could always count on my mother to keep things in perspective. Everything happened so fast at the convention—only a few hours separated President Ford's invitation to join the ticket from my introduction to a national television audience. The acceptance speech I gave on that occasion isn't likely to be chiseled in granite. Nevertheless, I got off a few decent one-liners at the expense of the opposition; maybe even changed a few votes in the crucial farm belt and among disaffected Reagan supporters. Or so I thought. By the time I finished, the adrenaline was really pumping. Returning to the holding room just off the convention floor, I ran into my mother.

"How did I do?" I asked her.

"You usually do better," she said.

Although my oratorical skills have never been confused with those of a Lincoln or a Churchill, I've at least avoided the fate of Warren G. Harding, the Ohio politician who invented the word "bloviate" to describe his unique platform style—a lumpish mix of spread-eagle patriotism, numbing alliteration, sentences that didn't parse, and phrases that didn't soar.

Harding's contemporary H. L. Mencken feasted on what he called Gamalielese (taken from Harding's biblical middle name, Gamaliel). To Mencken a typical Harding speech was reminiscent of "a string of wet sponges . . . tattered washing on the line . . . of stale bean soup, of college yells, of dogs barking idiotically through endless nights. It is so bad that a sort of grandeur creeps into it . . . it is rumble and bumble, flap and doodle, balder and dash."

Ouch.

If you're a regular C-SPAN viewer like me, you may be forgiven for thinking that most members of Congress act as if they're being paid by the word. Don't judge us too harshly—how would *you* like to think of something original to say every year on Lincoln's Birthday or at Boy Scout inductions or when called upon to address that bipartisan terror, the college commencement. Anyone who has ever attended a graduation knows they are mostly held in hot, stuffy gymnasiums full of kids who can't wait to graduate and parents who can't bear the thought of all those loan vouchers. At best, they're marked by equal amounts of inspiration and perspiration. When delivering a commencement speech I always begin by comparing the role of the speaker to that of a corpse at a funeral. You can't hold the event without one, but nobody expects you to say very much.

☆ ☆ ☆

A heckler once tossed a cabbage at William Howard Taft during a political speech. He paused, peered at the vegetable, and then placidly said, "Ladies and gentlemen, I see that one of my opponents has lost its head."

☆

Woodrow Wilson remarked, "The wisest thing to do with a fool is to encourage him to hire a hall and discourse to his fellow citizens. Nothing chills nonsense like exposure to the air."

☆

At a ceremony for the laying of a cornerstone, President Calvin Coolidge turned a spadeful of earth and then remained silent. Clearly, the gathering expected him to speak. The emcee whispered to him that a few words would be fitting.

Coolidge looked over the upturned earth and said, "That's a fine fish worm."

☆

Will Rogers was a particular favorite of Americans in the 1920s. Among his fans was Calvin Coolidge, whom Washington wags dubbed "The Great Stone Face." The comedian reciprocated, explaining not long after the celebrated Scopes "monkey trial" that "Coolidge is a better example of evolution than either Bryan or [Clarence] Darrow, for he knows when not to talk, which is the biggest asset the monkey possesses over the human."

☆

No one in the twentieth century marshaled the English language better than Winston Churchill. Presented with an official document of stupefying verbosity, he protested, "This paper, by its very length, defends itself against the risk of being read."

Not surprisingly, Churchill had no use for bureaucrats who scorned old, plain words, replacing poor people with "lower income group" and substituting "accommodation units" for homes. On the floor of the House of Commons one day, he startled fellow MPs by exploding in song: "Accommodation unit, sweet

accommodation unit, there's no place like accommodation unit."

In 1914, when Winston Churchill was First Lord of
the Admiralty, his forthrightness and outspokenness
attracted many critics. One of his most blunt critics
was Lord Charles Beresford. Churchill remarked,
"He can best be described as one of those orators
who, before they get up, do not know what they are
going to say; when they are speaking, do not know
what they are saying; and, when they have sat down,
do not know what they have said."

One evening, when Churchill was addressing an
audience in America, a gushing woman asked him,
"Doesn't it thrill you, Mr. Churchill, to know that
every time you make a speech the hall is packed to
overflowing?"

"It's quite flattering," Churchill replied, "but
whenever I feel this way I always remember that if
instead of making a political speech I was being
hanged, the crowd would be twice as big."

Churchill's advice to banquet speakers: "Say what you have to say and the first time you come to a sentence with a grammatical ending, sit down!"

Churchill entertained no illusions about his reprobate son Randolph, especially as far as the younger man's oratorical powers were concerned. "He has big guns but too little ammunition," Churchill complained. Randolph gave as well as he got. On hearing then Vice President Richard Nixon lavish praise on the elder Churchill's brilliant unrehearsed speechmaking, Randolph smiled and said, "My father has spent the best years of his life writing his extemporaneous speeches."

☆

Franklin Roosevelt was asked in 1938 to address the Daughters of the American Revolution. He opened his speech: "Fellow immigrants . . ."

☆

Adlai Stevenson once said, "The sound of tireless voices is the price we pay for the right to hear the music of our own opinions."

☆

In 1952, Richard Nixon remarked, "No TV performance takes such careful preparation as an off-the-cuff talk."

☆

On numerous occasions, Lyndon Johnson repeated this remark about two kinds of speeches: "The Mother Hubbard speech, which, like the garment, covers everything but touches nothing; and the French bathing suit speech, which covers only the essential points."

LBJ speechwriter Bob Hardesty recalls a day in 1966 when he and a fellow wordsmith were summoned to the Oval Office to be introduced to a long-time Johnson friend as "the best speechwriters any President ever had."

This was pretty heady stuff for a newly hired staffer. Hardesty swelled with pride at such recognition—until he heard Johnson explain why he held such a high opinion of the two writers and their talents: "They're not temperamental," said LBJ. "They don't miss deadlines. And they don't get drunk the night before a major speech."

☆

Former Minnesota senator Eugene McCarthy once remarked, "It's dangerous for a national candidate to say things that people might remember."

☆

When Hubert Humphrey was asked to limit a commencement speech to twelve minutes, he said, "The last time I spoke for only twelve minutes was when I said hello to my mother."

Humphrey explained his unbridled loquacity thusly: "It's just glands."

☆

Barry Goldwater, on Hubert Humphrey's celebrated loquacity: "Hubert has been clocked at 275 words a minute with gusts up to 340."

☆

Muriel Humphrey told her husband, "Hubert, a speech, to be immortal, doesn't have to be eternal."

☆

At the Women's Leadership Forum in July 1996, President Clinton said, "Sometimes I hate to be last, you know. The very first speech I ever gave as a public official, twenty years ago, January 1977, I was Attorney General. I went to a Rotary Club installation banquet. It's one of those deals that start at 6:30 P.M.; there were five hundred people there. Everybody in the crowd but four people got introduced; they went home mad. I got up to talk at a quarter to 10 P.M. and the guy that introduced me was the only person there more nervous than me, and the first words out of his mouth were: 'You know, we could stop here and have had a very nice evening.' "

Hecklers interrupted Clinton's speech in Denver in October 1996. "Look," he said, "you shouldn't be too upset about that. You know what Mark Twain said about that? He said every dog needs a few fleas. Now, I'll admit, I've had a few more than I wanted. But Mark Twain said every dog needs a few fleas because they keep him from worrying so much about being a dog.

"Which reminds me of my other favorite dog story. This guy is going down the highway and he sees this sign that says, 'George Jones, Veterinarian-Taxidermist. Either way, you get your dog back.' "

☆

Gerald Ford deprecated his own speechmaking abilities by telling of a visit to Omaha, where a sweet little old lady approached the future President at a post-address reception. "I hear you spoke here tonight," she told Ford.

"Oh, it was nothing," said Ford modestly.

"Yes," nodded the elderly woman, "that's what I heard."

Campaigning

───────────── ★ ─────────────

ONE OF MY FAVORITE stories about the campaign trail involves Abraham Lincoln's first race for Congress. Lincoln's Democrat opponent was a Methodist minister named Peter Cartwright, who was not above engaging in a bit of negative campaigning by contrasting his own fervor with his opponent's frequent absence from church. At one point in the campaign, Lincoln attended a gathering at which Cartwright preached a hellfire-and-brimstone sermon, concluding with an invitation for all those who desired to go to heaven to stand. Not surprisingly, a healthy portion of the congregation rose.

Next, Cartwright shouted, "All those who do not wish to go to hell will stand!" This time, the entire audience rose—but one. Cartwright saw his opening. "I observe that many of you accepted my invitation to give their hearts to God and go to heaven," he declared. "I further observed that all but one of you indicated an aversion to going to hell. The sole exception is Mr. Lincoln, who failed to respond to either invitation. May I inquire of you, Mr. Lincoln, where you are going?"

"Brother Cartwright asks me directly where I am going," said Lincoln. "Well, I'll tell you: I am going to Congress."

And so he did. Now, as then, the campaign trail tests a candidate's mettle, his character, his patience, and his stomach. Most of all, however, it tests his funny bone. In fact, when President Ford asked me to be his running mate in 1976, I asked my old friend Lyn Nofziger to join the Dole campaign team, and he readily agreed. "We won't win," he told a friend presciently. "But we'll have a lot of fun."

Fun is in the eye of the beholder. If I thought war was chaotic, it was nothing compared to my first run for national office. In the course of a single day, our press bus got stuck coming out of a tunnel in Boston, I spent a full hour stranded at a horse farm in Lexington, Kentucky, and I rode around an empty stadium next to an American Legion-sponsored carnival in New Jersey. I think even Lyn left to play the midway games.

My 1996 campaign also had its share of lighter moments—and it might surprise you when I say that one of them was when I fell off the stage in Chico, California. (I continue to insist that this was my attempt at "crowd surfing.") When Bill Daley fainted at the post-1996 election White House announcement of his appointment as Secretary of Commerce, I wrote to him to compliment him on his ability to fall off a stage on live national television. And I still kid President Bush that he got his idea to jump from a plane only after he saw me jump from a stage.

☆ ☆ ☆

"If you think too much about being reelected, it is very difficult to be worth reelecting."
—WOODROW WILSON

☆

Harry Truman once mused, "In most of my campaigns, I find it best not to mention my opponent by name because, by doing so, it just gives him the chance to get into the headlines."

Truman recalled, "Herbert Hoover once ran on the slogan 'Two cars in every garage!' Apparently the Republican candidate this year is running on the slogan 'Two families in every garage.' "

☆

The brilliant rogue Huey P. Long rarely let the truth get in the way of a good stump speech. Campaigning in heavily Catholic southern Louisiana, Long invariably began each speech by declaring, "When I was a boy, I would get up at six o'clock in the morning on Sunday, and I would hitch our old horse up to the buggy and I would take my Catholic grandparents to Mass. I would bring them home, and at ten o'clock I would hitch the old horse up again, and I would take my Baptist grandparents to church."

Not surprisingly, such evidence of youthful piety had a profound effect on Long's audiences. One night a local political boss who had gone out of his way to remind the candidate about the preponderance of Catholic voters in southern Louisiana expressed admiration for Long's devout conduct. "Why, Huey, you've been holding out on us," he added teasingly. "I didn't know you had any Catholic grandparent."

"Don't be a damn fool," replied Huey. "We didn't even have a horse."

☆

On the tone of Eisenhower's 1956 presidential campaign, Adlai Stevenson remarked, "The General dedicated himself so many times, he must feel like the cornerstone of a public building."

Stevenson also remarked, "The hardest thing about any political campaign is how to win without proving that you are unworthy of winning."

Informed by academics that he enjoyed "the support of all thinking Americans," Stevenson joked, "That's not enough. I'm going to need a majority."

☆

Throughout the 1960 campaign, one of the issues that John Kennedy continually faced was the accusation that he lacked the necessary experience to bechange President. In a political speech in Minneapolis in October 1960, Kennedy had this to say:

"Ladies and gentlemen, the outstanding news story of this week was not the events of the United Nations or even the presidential campaign. It was a story coming out of my own city of Boston that Ted Williams of the Boston Red Sox had retired from baseball. It seems that at forty-two, he was too old. It shows that perhaps experience isn't enough."

"There is no city in the United States," Kennedy said, "in which I get a warmer welcome and fewer votes than Columbus, Ohio."

In February 1961, Kennedy told the National Industrial Conference Board in Washington, "It would be premature to ask for your support in the next election, and it would be inaccurate to thank you for it in the past."

☆

During his Senate campaign in 1964, Robert Kennedy told an audience in New York City, "People say

I am ruthless. I am not ruthless. And if I find the man who is calling me ruthless, I shall destroy him."

☆

Explaining his 1964 presidential candidacy, Barry Goldwater said, "I'm too young to retire and too old to go back to work."

One of Goldwater's favorite stunts during the 1964 campaign was to poke his fingers through a pair of lensless black-rimmed glasses and proclaim, "These glasses are just like Lyndon Johnson's programs. They look good, but they don't work."

During a Senate campaign speech in the Catskills in 1964, Robert Kennedy went after the Republican nominee: "The Catskills were immortalized by Washington Irving. He wrote of a man who fell asleep and awoke in another era. The only other area that can boast of such a man is Phoenix, Arizona . . . Barry Goldwater wants to give control of nuclear weapons to commanders in the field. Now, that's my idea of high adventure. General Eisenhower says that he could live with a Goldwater administration. Well, I suppose he'd have as good a chance as anyone else."

★

Massachusetts senator Edward Kennedy remembers, "I ran for the Senate at a very young age, and one of the issues used by the opponents was that I had never worked a day in my life. One day I was going through one of the factories in my state to meet the workers. And I will never forget the fellow who came up to me, shook my hand, and said, 'Mr. Kennedy, I understand that you have never worked a day in your life. Let me tell you, you haven't missed a thing.' "

★

At the 1966 Gridiron Dinner, Hubert Humphrey remembered the 1964 campaign. "As most of you remember, it was a very clean campaign, without the usual name-calling that goes with a presidential election. To this day, I have a great deal of respect for Barry Goldwater and his running mate, what's-his-name."

★

The great Illinois senator Everett Dirksen noted, "During a political campaign, everyone is concerned with what a candidate will do on this or that question if he is elected, except the candidate; he's too busy wondering what he'll do if he isn't elected."

★

Democratic Wisconsin senator William Proxmire told this story when he spoke in Chicago: "In Milwaukee, we haven't quite learned the art of government as you have learned it here in Chicago. You have a certain skill and a certain touch, which we are working on, but we haven't quite achieved it yet. Just recently, I was shaking hands with some of my constituents and a fellow came up to me and said, 'Proxmire, I have been for you from the beginning. All those times you ran for governor, I voted for you every time. I voted for you when you ran for Senate. I have always voted for you.'

"I said, 'Wonderful! What can I do for you?'

"He said, 'Well, Senator, there is something you can do for me. I am trying to get my citizenship.'"

★

Referring to the February 1984 Democratic presidential primary debate in New Hampshire, President Reagan told *Newsweek,* "There were so many candidates on the platform that there were not enough promises to go around."

☆

House Speaker Tip O'Neill once observed, "As we all know, the truth is a frequent casualty in the heat of an election campaign."

☆

At a black tie dinner in Washington in 1987, Senator Jay Rockefeller took the podium to address a crowd that had paid $500 a plate for the evening's meager meal. Rockefeller had recently won a close Senate race in which he had spent a considerable amount of his personal fortune. "Some of you might feel cheated, paying five hundred bucks for a lousy chicken dinner," he said. "But just think about me: I spent ten million dollars to get here."

☆

Michael Dukakis said in 1988, "I had to run for President to find out my eyebrows had become a status symbol." He grinned. "If you can't remember my name, and can't pronounce it, just remember—go for the guy with the bushy eyebrows."

☆

When Jesse Jackson was asked to react to the frequent comment that the country is not ready for a black President, he told this story:

"Three Iowa farmers were discussing the bank's attempt to take their farms by foreclosing their mortgages.

"The first farmer said, 'I like the way that fellow Jesse Jackson talks. He knows a lot about the issues, but he's black.'

"The second farmer said, 'I like him, too. I like the way he joined the farmers' picket line at the bank last week. I like the way he brought the hostage back from Syria. But you're right, he is black.'

"The third farmer interrupted: 'I don't think you two understand. The guy who is taking our farms is white.' "

☆

Dan Quayle, often the butt of jokes, gives as well as he gets. Quayle likes to tell of his first campaign for Congress back in 1976, when he went up to a prospective voter in New Haven, Indiana, stuck out his hand, and announced, "I'm Dan Quayle from Huntington. I'm running for Congress, and I'd like you to vote for me."

The man put his head down and mumbled, "Well, I was going to vote for you until I found out that you were a lawyer." Quayle quickly recovered. "I am a lawyer," he acknowledged, "but I don't practice law."

The voter perked up his ears and said, "Well, what do you do?"

"I publish a newspaper," said Quayle.

"Heck, that's worse," said the voter.

☆

President Clinton's fondness for food has been the subject of many jokes—including some by himself. In 1994 he cracked, "People say to me, 'Like Harry Truman, if you can't stand the heat, get out of the kitchen.' That's the only room in the house I don't want to leave."

Politicians

——————— ⭐ ———————

POLITICIANS ARE ACCUSED of many things. The charge that we live in another world, one remote from the popular culture, is one that usually sticks. But you shouldn't blame us for *trying*. After hearing my daughter Robin, then a high school student, enthuse over a British rock band that was planning a visit to the United States, I took it upon myself to write the British Embassy in Washington to see if the band might surprise her and her classmates by playing at their school. Regrettably, I was informed, the Beatles would be unable to include Robin's school on their forthcoming American tour.

In other ways, living with a politician poses curious tests. Before seeking permission to have her ears pierced, my daughter carefully researched and wrote a decision memo similar to those that came to me every day from members of my congressional staff. At the bottom of the page she placed two boxes to be checked, one marked "Yes," the other "No." The morning after Robin presented me with the memo, she woke to find the paper slipped under her door, with a third option—"Maybe"—scribbled in by her father.

Right about now the ageless Senator Strom Thurmond is probably facing similar requests from his children. Born in 1902, Strom has served in the United States Senate since 1954. As the oldest senator in U.S. history, Strom is often the first one on the floor in the morning and the last one to leave at night. Having been the frequent target of cracks about my own age during the 1996 campaign, I wouldn't joke about Strom's if he didn't like it. Yet no one laughs harder than he does.

Take the celebration of the Capitol's two hundredth anniversary in 1993. This occasioned a lengthy, unsuccessful attempt to find the cornerstone laid by George Washington in 1793. I couldn't resist. "Strom is the only person who was there at the time," I remarked, "and he's not telling." In front of a bipartisan crowd of nearly a thousand admirers gathered for Strom's ninetieth birthday party, I let it be known that everyone in attendance had one thing in common. "We all served at one time or another as an intern for Strom."

When his turn came to speak, Strom noted how, all evening, people had been coming up to him to express the hope that they would be present for his hundredth birthday. To which he replied, forthrightly enough, that if they ate right and exercised regularly he couldn't see any reason why they shouldn't be around to see it.

☆ ☆ ☆

"The more you read and observe about this politics thing, you've got to admit that each party is worse than the other."

—WILL ROGERS

☆

Adlai Stevenson rarely shied away from the use of self-deprecating humor. He was especially fond of telling about the Democratic convention at which a very pregnant pro-Stevenson delegate carried a sign proclaiming, "Adlai's the Man!"

☆

President Taft joked about his long career in public service. Asked by a newspaperman why he got started so young, the good-natured Taft answered, "Like every well-trained Ohio man, I always had my plate the right side up when offices were falling."

☆

Woodrow Wilson once remarked, "A friend of mine says that every man who takes office in Washington either grows or swells, and when I give a man an office, I watch him carefully to see whether he is swelling or growing."

Wilson maintained a healthy sense of humor about the sometimes inscrutable ways of professional politicians. As governor of New Jersey, Wilson received word that one of the state's United States senators had just died. Within minutes he got a second call, this one from an ambitious pol, who informed Wilson that "I would like to take the senator's place."

"Well," replied Wilson, "you may quote me as saying that is perfectly agreeable to me if agreeable to the undertaker."

☆

Herbert Hoover liked to tell of the child who asked him for not one but three autographs. When the former President asked why, he was informed crisply that "it takes two of yours to get one of Babe Ruth's."

☆

While passing through the park, Calvin Coolidge was asked by his companion if the man they had just passed on horseback was Senator Borah, who was not one of Coolidge's favorite politicians. "Can't be," Coolidge drawled. "The senator and the horse were going in the same direction."

☆

In a speech to the House of Commons, Churchill elucidated his feelings about then Treasurer Ramsay MacDonald. "I remember when I was a child being taken to the celebrated Barnum's circus, which contained an exhibition of freaks and monstrosities, but the exhibit on the program which I desired to see was the one described as 'The Boneless Wonder.' My parents judged that spectacle would be too revolting and demoralizing for my youthful eyes, and I have waited fifty years to see 'The Boneless Wonder' sitting on the Treasury Bench."

Churchill, on what it takes to be a politician: "It's the ability to foretell what will happen tomorrow, next month, and next year — and to explain afterward why it did not happen."

Churchill, on Sir Stafford Cripps, the rather snooty Chancellor of the Exchequer: "He has all the virtues I dislike and none of the vices I admire." And on Prime Minister Clement Attlee: "He's a sheep in sheep's clothing."

☆

Teddy Roosevelt got off one of the most famous insults in American political history, when, as Assistant Secretary of the Navy, he said of the pacific William McKinley, "He has no more backbone than a chocolate éclair."

On another occasion, Roosevelt disparaged McKinley, whose sensitivity to popular opinion was legendary, by claiming the President had his ear so close to the ground that it was full of grasshoppers.

☆

Along with Franklin Roosevelt's sense of timing went the artist's need to dominate. Members of his own staff enjoyed imagining what might happen if their boss died and went to heaven. Greeted cordially by St. Peter, Roosevelt requested a grand heavenly choir to mark the occasion of his arrival.

"I want ten thousand sopranos," he told Peter, who gladly complied. "I want ten thousand contraltos." Peter promised to do his best.

How many basses would be required? asked the divine gatekeeper. "Oh, that's all right," answered Roosevelt with a smile. "I'm planning to sing that part myself."

☆

Truman offered the following definition: "A statesman is a politician who's been dead for ten or fifteen years."

☆

Remembering the 1948 presidential campaign, Speaker of the House Tip O'Neill told the PBS program *The Great Upset of '48*, "I took my own informal, politician's poll. I talked to fifty-six people. All fifty-six said that they didn't think that Truman could win, but all fifty-six said they were voting for Truman."

☆

Truman on Nixon: "[He] is one of the few men in the history of this country to run for high office talking out of both sides of his mouth at the same time and lying out of both sides."

☆

Barry Goldwater is known to be a most proficient photographer. He once took a good photo of JFK and sent it to him for an autograph. The picture was returned with this inscription: "For Barry Goldwater, whom I urge to follow the career for which he has shown so much talent—photography. From his friend John Kennedy."

☆

In August 1960, John Kennedy remarked, "Mr. Nixon may be very experienced in kitchen debates. So are a great many other married men I know."

JFK privately referred to Senator Everett Dirksen as "The Wizard of Ooze."

Kennedy made this witty observation about the American public's impression of politics: "Mothers may still want their sons to grow up to be President, but, according to a famous Gallup poll of some years ago, some 73 percent do not want them to become politicians in the process."

☆

Tip O'Neill remembered, "Jack Kennedy . . . played the game of politics by his own rules. . . . During his early years in politics, he hated shaking hands, which was highly unusual in a city where some politicians had been known to shake hands with fire hydrants and wave to telephone poles."

☆

When Nelson Rockefeller first decided to run for governor of New York in 1958, he went to see the state's former Republican governor Tom Dewey, who slapped his knee and laughed out loud before declaring, "Nelson, you're a great guy, but you couldn't get elected dogcatcher in New York."

The voters proved Dewey wrong, but the passage of time—and innumerable bond issues—didn't make Dewey any more enamored of Rockefeller's big spending, high taxing style of governing. "I like you, Nelson," Dewey once remarked to his liberal successor, "but I don't think I can afford you."

☆

It was no secret that Nelson Rockefeller and New York City mayor John Lindsay didn't get along. "You've already said that the mayor is incompetent running this city," a reporter once said to Rockefeller.

"That wasn't the word I used," protested the governor.

"What was the word you used?" the reporter demanded.

"Inept," said Rockefeller.

Nelson Rockefeller was often the master of unwitting humor. At one point during his 1968 presidential campaign, he summoned an advance man to his motel room.

"Joe, sit down," said the candidate. "I'm worried about expenses in this campaign."

"Yes, sir," replied the advance man. "It's an expensive business."

Rockefeller plunged ahead. "Now, I like Oreo cookies. But I only eat three or four," he said, rummaging in a wastebasket for an empty Oreo package. Then he reached into a dish piled high with the offending cookies. "Here you've got two dozen." Rockefeller started to drop the Oreos into the empty package. "Can't we get a refund on packages we don't use?"

★

Ronald Reagan told this story about Lyndon Johnson as Vice President: "Johnson was coming off the

Senate floor when he ran into a reporter for the *New York Times.* Johnson grabbed him, shouted 'You, I've been looking for you,' pulled him into his office, and began a long harangue about something or other.

"About halfway through, he scribbled a note on a scrap of paper, buzzed his secretary, and gave it to her. She was back in a minute with another note. He glanced at it while he talked, and threw it away.

"And eventually, the reporter got out, but as he left the outer office, he saw the note that Johnson had written lying on the secretary's desk. It said, 'Who's this guy I'm talking to anyway?' "

☆

Ronald Reagan once said, "Keeping up with Governor Brown's promises is like reading *Playboy* magazine while your wife turns the pages."

☆

During Reagan's triumphant campaign for the 1980 Republican nomination: "I haven't had Jimmy Carter's experience. I wouldn't be caught dead with it."

A famous Reagan assessment: "Depression is when you're out of work. A recession is when your neighbor is out of work. Recovery is when Carter's out of work."

Reagan on his 1980 opponent: "I had a dream the other night. I dreamed that Jimmy Carter came to me and asked why I wanted his job. I told him I didn't want his job. I want to be President."

"Carter was supposed to go on *60 Minutes* to talk about his accomplishments, but that left him with fifty-nine minutes to fill," said Reagan.

Reagan on Carter: "The President had ordered there be no hard liquor in the White House. And now we find out some of the White House has been smoking pot. This is the first administration we can honestly say is high and dry."

When Carter refused to join the debate between Reagan and John Anderson, Reagan explained:

"President Carter has been debating candidate Carter for the past three and a half years—and losing."

☆

Gerald Ford once quipped, "Ronald Reagan doesn't dye his hair—he's just prematurely orange."

☆

Remembering the 1972 election on PBS's *America's Political Parties—the Democrats,* Tip O'Neill said that Senator George McGovern was "nominated by the cast of *Hair.*"

☆

Running against Clinton in 1992, Bush said, "[Bill Clinton] says he wants to tax the rich, but, folks, he defines 'rich' as anyone who has a job. You've heard of the separation of powers. My opponent practices a different theory: 'The power of separations.' Government has the power to separate you from your wallet."

☆

In an address to the Washington Press Club Foundation in 1995, the late congressman Sonny Bono said of Texas Republican senator Phil Gramm, "I wanted to be a senator. I went to one of his affairs and he said something like 'You can't eat corn if you ain't a pig.' I said to my wife, 'What the hell does that mean?' "

☆

Republican congressman Michael P. Flanagan from Chicago was overwhelmingly defeated for re-election in 1996. Asked what was the most astonishing thing he learned in Washington, Flanagan joked, "Newt [Gingrich] really doesn't wear a toupee. That's really his hair."

☆

Alan Simpson of Wyoming was one of my closest friends and advisers in the Senate. He is also one of the funniest people I know. Many of his jokes aren't suitable for family reading, but his typical bluntness can be seen in this line: "We have the same percentage of lightweights in Congress as you have in your hometown. After all, it's representative government."

Al also said, "If you don't know who you are before you get to Washington, D.C., this is a poor place to find out."

☆

No book on political wit would be complete without a story from the late Speaker of the House, Tip O'Neill. Here, in his own words, is one of Tip's most repeated stories: An Irishman went into the local bank to get a loan to buy a house. The Yankee banker looked up the record of the Irishman's bank account, then he looked over the application for the loan, and then he addressed the applicant. "I have a standard test," he said. "I have one glass eye and one real eye. I'll give you the loan if you can tell me which is my glass eye and which is my real eye."

The Irishman studied each of the banker's eyes carefully. "The glass eye is the left eye," he finally said.

"You're correct," said the banker. "But how could you tell?"

"It was easy," said the Irishman. "The left eye had warmth in it."

Defeat

---- ⭐ ----

HENRY CLAY UNSUCCESSFULLY sought the White House three times. Today he is remembered for saying he would rather be right than President. Henry Clay was his own spin doctor. Apparently Pat Buchanan's thinking of making his own third attempt in 2000. You can already hear his post-primary credo: I'd rather be far right than President. Many people may not know it, but I first ran for President in 1980. Looking back, that year's campaign represented one of my biggest political jokes. Remember the famous debate between Ronald Reagan and the publisher of the *Nashua Telegraph* over who had paid for the microphone? Reagan won hands down, as he usually did whenever a microphone was involved. Although George Bush looked pretty uncomfortable sharing the stage with the Great Communicator that night, he had it easier than the rest of us aging group of chorus boys in the star attraction's shadow.

In the 1996 campaign, of course, age became an issue. Apparently too many New Hampshire voters mistook me for the Old Man of the Mountain. In between, of course, I lost the 1988 Granite State primary to George Bush. My lashing out at Bush on the night of the primary would linger in popular memory long after everyone forgot the last-minute negative ads run by the Bush campaign which had prompted my outburst. For many voters, it brought back Richard Nixon's angry "last press conference" following his defeat in the 1962 California gubernatorial contest.

Later years would afford Nixon unparalleled triumphs and public disgrace. Yet he never gave in and he never gave up. He handled defeat with a grace born of personal character that his harshest critics refused to acknowledge. I will never forget the June day in 1993 when we buried Pat Nixon in the magnificent rose gardens at the Nixon Library and Museum in Yorba Linda, California. Television viewers saw an old man walking unsteadily, bowed by the weight of his sorrow. The three hundred invited guests saw something else. As one of the eulogists at the simple service, I couldn't begin to match the moving talk that President Nixon himself delivered inside the library, away from television's prying eye.

Among other things, Nixon told how much he and Pat had enjoyed being grandparents. He recalled their youngest granddaughter, Jennie Eisenhower, asking Mrs. Nixon the first time how she wished to be addressed. After rejecting "Grandmother" as too formal and "Grandma" as too aged for her liking, Pat suggested to the little girl that she call her "Ma."

Jennie next put the same question to her famous grandfather. "Oh, you can call me anything," said Nixon, "because I've been called everything."

I wasn't the only one in the room struggling to control my emotions. A few feet away, dabbing at his eyes with a handkerchief, stood George McGovern, Nixon's 1972 election opponent. Asked by a reporter why he should honor the wife of a man whose alleged dirty tricks had denied him the presidency, George replied, "You can't keep on campaigning forever."

★ ★ ★

There was probably no classier loser in American politics than my fellow Kansan Alf Landon. In November 1936, voters overwhelmingly reelected Franklin Roosevelt; the GOP ticket carried just two states, Vermont and Maine. Fortunately, Landon told reporters afterward, being a Kansan he was prepared for the worst. "The Kansas tornado is an old story," he went on. "But let me tell you of one. It swept away first the barn, then the outbuildings, then it picked up the dwelling and scattered it all over the landscape.

"As the funnel cloud went twisting its way out of sight, leaving nothing behind but splinters, the farmer's wife came to. She was astonished to find her husband laughing uncontrollably.

" 'What are you laughing at, you darned old fool?' " she demanded.

" 'The completeness of it,' said the farmer."

☆

William Howard Taft didn't enjoy his four years in the White House, nor the bitter three-way contest in 1912 leading to his defeat at the hands of Woodrow Wilson and Theodore Roosevelt. Taft did not remain bitter for long. Within days of the voting, he found what solace he could in his dismal showing, telling friends that he took some consolation in knowing that no man in American history had ever been elected ex-President by such an overwhelming majority.

☆

Just after Winston Churchill's defeat in 1945, the King offered him the Order of the Garter, causing Churchill to wonder aloud: "Why should I accept the

Order of the Garter from His Majesty, when the people have just given me the order of the boot?"

After the defeat, Churchill's wife tried to cheer him up. "It might be a blessing in disguise," she told him. "At the moment," he replied, "it seems quite effectively disguised."

☆

After his defeat in the 1952 presidential election, Adlai Stevenson recalled, "Down the street, someone asked me, as I came in, how I felt, and I was reminded of a story that a fellow townsman of ours used to tell—Abraham Lincoln. They asked him how he felt once after an unsuccessful election. He said he felt like a little boy who stubbed his toe in the dark. He said that he was too old to cry, but it hurt too much to laugh."

☆

Shortly after President Kennedy's famous inauguration in 1961, Nixon and presidential aide Ted Sorensen met. Their conversation turned to Kennedy's inaugural address.

"I wish I had said some of those things," Nixon said.

"What part?" Sorensen asked, justifiably proud of his speechwriting prowess. "That part about 'Ask not what your country can do for you . . .'?"

"No," replied Nixon. "The part that starts, 'I do solemnly swear.' "

☆

In what might be the motto of those who sought the presidency and lost, Ted Kennedy once said, "Frankly, I don't mind not being President. I just mind that someone else is."

☆

Acknowledging his loss in the 1976 presidential primaries, Morris Udall said, "The voters have spoken—the bastards!"

When he was asked in 1980 whether he would consider running for President again, Udall said, "If nominated, I will run to Mexico; if elected, I will fight extradition."

★

Soon after leaving the White House, Gerald Ford and his wife, Betty, flew to Houston for a fund-raising dinner honoring the memory of Vince Lombardi. It was a commitment Ford had agreed to while still in office. As Ford brooded over his loss to Jimmy Carter, he wondered if dinnergoers might not feel let down. "They thought they'd be getting a sitting President," he told Betty.

"Don't worry, darling," said the irreverent Mrs. Ford. "It is me they're coming to see."

★

By its nature, politics is a competitive business, as seen by Jimmy Carter's conclusion: "Show me a good loser, and I'll show you a loser."

The Presidency

───────── ☆ ─────────

I HAVE COME TO the conclusion that the major part of the work of a President is to increase the gate receipts of expositions and fairs and bring tourists to town." That was William Howard Taft's first-person analysis of the job that is now frequently described as being "the leader of the free world."

There is no doubt that the duties and responsibilities of the office have changed a great deal since Taft's term in office, but one thing that has not changed is the public's delight at poking fun at Presidents and the presidency. And I believe it's not just a coincidence that the two most successful Presidents of this century—Franklin Roosevelt and Ronald Reagan—are also the two who possessed the healthiest sense of humor about themselves and their job.

And if Presidents should laugh at themselves, so, too, should the American people. I've always believed in the truth of the old saying that "America is

great because anyone can grow up to be President."
But I also believe that America is great because anyone can grow up and make fun of the President. During my three and a half decades on Capitol Hill, I
had the privilege of serving under nine Presidents,
and I suppose I poked fun at all of them, at one time
or another. Indeed, one of my most often repeated
quips was the one I made when former Presidents
Carter, Ford, and Nixon stood by each other at a
White House event. "There they are," I said. "See no
evil, hear no evil, and . . . evil." (By the way, I
know that President Nixon—who once paid me the
ultimate compliment by saying that my comedic timing was better than Bob Hope's—saw the humor in
this line.) But even while I was joking about the men
who have served in the Oval Office, I never have and
never will show any disrespect for the office of the
presidency.

While never being one to engage in "what-if's," I
am often asked as I travel around the country what
type of President I would have been—or in the words
of Norm MacDonald, who impersonated me so well
on the television show *Saturday Night Live,* Bob Dole
is often asked as Bob Dole travels around the country
what type of President Bob Dole would have been.

The best way I can respond to that question is to
go back to the very beginning of my political career,
when I was elected to the Kansas House of Represen-

tatives in 1950, and a reporter asked me what my agenda would be. "I'm going to sit and watch for a couple of days," I told him, "and then I'll stand up for what is right." Standing up for what I believe is right has been my agenda throughout my public service career, and it would have been my agenda in the White House.

But I have always been one who preferred looking to the future over rehashing the past. And the question I am most often asked about the future is "Who do you think the Republican Party will nominate for the presidency in the year 2000." And my answer is "I don't know, but I predict that she will win."

☆ ☆ ☆

Woodrow Wilson once reflected, "There are blessed intervals when I forget by one means or another that I am President of the United States."

Wilson was a man of acerbic wit. The former history professor observed of his less than brilliant successor that Warren G. Harding had a "bungalow mind." Asked to explain the phrase, Wilson pointed to his forehead and said, "No upper story."

☆

Calvin Coolidge saw his role as follows: "I always figured the American public wanted a solemn ass for President, so I went along with them."

Calvin Coolidge, a more talkative man than legend suggests, enjoyed regularly entertaining the half dozen or so reporters who made up the White House press corps in the 1920s. The President replied in the affirmative when a journalist asked if he was planning on attending the Sesquicentennial Exposition in Philadelphia. "Why are you going, Mr. President?" pressed the reporter. "As an exhibit," said Coolidge.

☆

In March 1909, William Howard Taft's inaugural had to be moved inside due to the worst blizzard to strike Washington in many years. "I've always said it would be a cold day when I get to be President of the United States," observed Taft.

☆

Making light of Republican criticism of his decision to seek an unprecedented fourth term in 1944, Franklin Delano Roosevelt quipped, "The first twelve years are the hardest."

Franklin D. Roosevelt got a good many laughs out of his opposition. Once told by a White House aide that Republican Wendell Willkie had his eye on the President's chair, FDR replied, mischievously, "Ah, but look what I've got on it."

☆

In a letter to his sister in 1947, Truman wrote, "All the President is, is a glorified public relations man who spends his time flattering, kissing, and kicking people to get them to do what they are supposed to do anyway."

☆

Truman reflected, "Any man who has had the job I've had and didn't have a sense of humor wouldn't still be here."

"If I hadn't been President of the United States," Truman once said, "I probably would have ended up a piano player in a bawdy house."

Truman's salty wit was never better displayed than when explaining his decision not to seek another term in 1952. By way of explanation, he quoted an epitaph from a cemetery in Tombstone, Arizona: "Here lies Jack Williams. He has done his damnedest."

⭐

In his 1961 State of the Union address, Eisenhower observed, "Unlike presidential administrations, problems rarely have terminal dates."

⭐

Adlai Stevenson observed, "They pick a President, and then for four years they pick on him."

"In America," Stevenson reflected, "any boy may become President, and I suppose that's just the risk he takes."

☆

Barry Goldwater once said ruefully, and I know how he feels, "It's a great country, where anybody can grow up to be President . . . except me."

☆

John F. Kennedy loathed giving long-winded explications of himself or the office of the presidency. When asked to discuss such matters, he would reply, "I have a nice home, the office is close by, and the pay is good."

☆

At a panel discussion featuring a number of men who had served as White House Chief of Staff, NBC correspondent John Chancellor asked each participant what he had done to prevent his boss, the President, from doing something really stupid.

Following an uncomfortable silence, Ted Sorensen, a veteran of the Kennedy White House, spoke up. "We didn't do too well in the first six months," said Sorensen. "You will recall the Bay of Pigs and a few other things. But we finally developed a formula that worked. What we did was to let President Kennedy get up a good head of steam, and then we would go up to him and say, 'You know, Mr. President, that's a terrific idea. That's exactly the way Dick Nixon would handle it.' "

☆

Maine Republican senator Margaret Chase Smith was once asked by a constituent, "What would you do if you woke up one morning and found yourself in the White House?"

Smith replied, "I would go to the President's wife and apologize, and then leave at once."

☆

Just before he assumed office, Ronald Reagan was briefed by his advisers on the many problems that the country faced. He joked, "I think I'll demand a recount."

Reagan regularly made a laughing matter out of his age. In 1987, he told one audience celebrating the Bicentennial of the Constitution, "History is no easy subject. Even in my day it wasn't, and we had so much less to learn then."

One of Ronald Reagan's favorite stories concerns an American and a Soviet citizen who were comparing their respective forms of government. "In my country," said the American, "I can walk into the Oval Office in the White House, and slam my fist on the desk, and say that I don't like the way Ronald Reagan is running the United States."

"Well," replied his Soviet counterpart, "I can do the same thing in the Politburo."

"You can?" asked the incredulous American.

"Certainly I can," came the response. "I can go

into Gorbachev's office, and slam my fist on his desk, and say that I don't like the way President Reagan is running the United States."

I recall the unforgettable day in the Reagan administration when an American plane shot down two Libyan jets, and the White House was engulfed in controversy because aides failed to wake the President in the middle of the night. The next day, Reagan got off a trademark quip: "I've laid down the law to everyone from now on about anything that happens that no matter what time it is I'm to be awakened, even if it's in the middle of a cabinet meeting."

☆

George Bush was one President who always kept his ego in check. When told that a company would be coming out with "presidential trading cards" for kids, he said, "I don't dare ask how many hundreds of George Bush cards you have to trade to get one Michael Jordan."

The Vice Presidency

———————☆———————

To JOKE ABOUT being Vice President seems almost redundant. It's a job no one campaigns for openly, no one turns down if offered, and no one emerges from unscathed. For most of his adult life Nelson Rockefeller told anyone who would listen that he wasn't cut out to be Vice President of anything. Yet he swallowed his reservations when Gerald Ford offered him the job.

When Rocky took himself out of the running for the 1976 nomination, there was widespread speculation over whom President Ford might choose to replace him. President Ford and his advisers delayed his decision until his nomination had been secured at the convention in Kansas City. I knew I was in the running, but didn't know I had been selected until Elizabeth and I heard a crowd of reporters descend upon our hotel room. A few minutes later, the phone rang and President Ford officially asked me to be his running mate. I thought it over for about one second before accepting.

Immediately after the convention, we flew to Russell, Kansas, for a community celebration. After the rally, my mother invited the President to her house for some refreshments. Unfortunately, when we arrived, the house was locked, no one had a key, and the spare was not hidden in its usual place. A crowd was gathering, and I was worried that President Ford was about ready to change his mind, when Elizabeth found the spare behind a drainpipe.

A spare hidden behind a drainpipe—I think if our first Vice President, John Adams, had been there, he would have thought that was a good description of the job he filled for eight years. In 1789, he wrote this withering analysis of the vice presidency: "My country has in its wisdom contrived for me the most insignificant office that ever the invention of man contrived or his imagination conceived."

☆ ☆ ☆

As Vice President, Coolidge lived in a suite at Washington's Willard Hotel on Pennsylvania Avenue. When fire broke out in the hotel one night, guests were ushered to safety in the lobby. After waiting for the all clear to be sounded, Coolidge lost his patience. Before he could head back upstairs, he was stopped by the fire warden, who demanded identification.

"I am the Vice President," said Coolidge indignantly. The warden was about to let him pass, before a second thought occurred to him.

"Vice President of what?" he asked.

"Vice President of the United States."

"Then get back here," said the fire warden. "I thought you were vice president of the hotel."

As presiding officer of the United States Senate, Vice President Calvin Coolidge declared his intention to master the rules governing the world's greatest deliberative body. This didn't take long, said Coolidge, who quickly discovered that the Senate has but one rule, which is that the Senate will do whatever it wants whenever it wants to.

☆

When Harry Truman was Vice President, he attended a photo session for a war bond relief drive at the White House. Secretary of State Edward Stettinius, Eleanor Roosevelt, and Bob Hope were posing for photographs, and when Truman kept trying to get into the shots, Hope became annoyed. Stettinius said, "Oh, Bob, do you know the Vice President?" Hope immediately apologized: "I'm sorry, Mr. Truman, I didn't recognize you." Truman said, "That's the best part of this job."

☆

After his failed attempt for the vice presidential nomination in 1956, JFK eschewed any future bids for the second-highest post. In 1958, when a friend assured him he was a shoo-in for the vice presidency in 1960, Kennedy amicably replied, "Let's not talk so much about vice. I'm against vice in any form."

☆

Lyndon Johnson had a fairly low opinion of the office of the vice presidency. "All Hubert needs over there," he once said, "is a gal to answer the phone and a pencil with an eraser on it."

Lyndon Johnson was just one in a long parade of unhappy Vice Presidents. His wife, Lady Bird, tried to make the best of the situation when she remarked, "At least we get our pictures in the papers."

☆

In August 1964, during the strained period before President Johnson announced his choice of a running mate, Hubert Humphrey waited patiently for Johnson's decision. Three days before the decision deadline, Humphrey was stopped in a hotel lobby by a local television interviewer. Nervously waving a microphone in his face, the interviewer asked tensely, "Senator, do you know anything? Are you nervous? Are you anxious? How are you holding up?"

"Obviously a lot better than you are," Humphrey replied calmly.

Humphrey commented on his choice to accept the vice presidential nomination in 1964 with a certain irony that was the hallmark of his creed. "I weighed the decision on the vice presidency very carefully. Not long, but carefully." While he wasn't certain what qualities he would bring to the office, he knew that "I didn't have . . . reluctance!"

☆

The celebrated actress Rosalind Russell, at a dinner with Humphrey, declared that the presidency was the most difficult job in the world. Humphrey insisted that the vice presidency was harder. "The President has only 190 million bosses," he explained. "The Vice President has 190 million *and one.*"

In 1966, at the annual Gridiron Dinner, Humphrey's hilarious address amply demonstrated a healthy sense of humor about himself. Describing his meeting with President Johnson just after he'd been selected as Johnson's running mate, Humphrey remembered: "The President [Johnson] looked at me and said, 'Hubert, do you think you can keep your mouth shut for the next four years?' I said, 'Yes, Mr. President,' and he said, 'There you go interrupting me again.' "

☆

As Vice President, not even Nelson Rockefeller could avoid the annual Gridiron Dinner. Called upon to speak for the GOP at the 1975 affair, Rocky declared that his selection proved the Ford White House to be an equal opportunity employer. He also made light of his prolonged confirmation hearings, with their embarrassing revelations of significant gifts to staff and friends. "I should have stuck by my grandfather's example," said Rockefeller. "He only gave away dimes."

☆

As Vice President, George Bush once said, "It's important for a Vice President not to upstage his boss, and you don't know how hard it has been to keep my charisma in check these last few years."

☆

Walter Mondale once said, "If you want to talk to somebody who's not busy, call the Vice President. I get plenty of time to talk to anybody about anything."

☆

Dan Quayle was fond of quoting his fellow Hoosier Vice President Thomas Marshall, who liked to tell of two brothers, one of whom went away to sea and the other became Vice President—and neither was ever heard from again.

The White House

---- ✩ ----

YOU WOULD THINK that as a symbol of American democracy, the White House would be above partisan politics. In fact, so often has the house been targeted for mudslinging, it's a wonder the walls are still white. In the nineteenth century, John Quincy Adams was denounced by opponents for purchasing a billiard table with public funds.

Martin Van Buren, an aristocratic figure who had the misfortune to preside over America's first Great Depression, was assailed on the floor of the House for living "in a palace as splendid as that of the Caesars." And when Van Buren bought some finger bowls for the state dining room, he was attacked for spending the people's cash on "foreign Fanny Kemble green finger cups, in which to wash his pretty, tapering, soft, white, lily fingers, after dining on fricandeau de veau and omelette soufflé" (whatever "fricandeau de veau" is).

In those days, the White House was less a bully pulpit than a political punching bag, with Congress withholding appropriations for upkeep and refurbishment when the executive failed to do its bidding. President James K. Polk, who banned Sabbath dancing and card parties, inspired Sam Houston to declare that the only problem with Polk was that he drank too much water. Later in the century, the Hayeses, Rutherford and Lucy, brought their own brand of family values to the place. In addition to nightly hymn singing, they practiced temperance with a vengeance. This led a wisecracking congressman who happened to visit the White House after Hayes won a crucial showdown on Capitol Hill to declare that at the ensuing celebration "the water flowed like wine."

More recently, Ronald and Nancy Reagan were derided by many when they restored some elegance to the White House furnishings—this despite the fact that they used private and not public funds. The courageous Mrs. Reagan would finally win over the Washington, D.C., media when she poked fun at herself at a Gridiron Dinner, dressed in an outrageous getup and singing a parody of the song "Second Hand Rose" entitled "Second Hand Clothes."

Elizabeth and I had hoped to have an opportunity to add our Kansas and North Carolina touches to the

White House beginning on January 20, 1997, but that was not to be. I did, however, have the chance to visit the White House three days earlier, when President Clinton honored me by presenting me with the Presidential Medal of Freedom. After President Clinton placed the medal around my neck, I began my remarks by saying, "I, Robert J. Dole, do solemnly swear . . . Sorry, wrong speech." I added that I had hoped that instead of a medal President Clinton would be giving me the key to the front door.

And I was honored to be the commencement speaker for the George Washington University Class of 1998. The large audience of over twenty thousand was seated on the White House Ellipse. I shared the following thoughts: "It was always a dream of mine to address a vast throng assembled on the Mall on a bright Washington day. I must confess, however, that I pictured it a little differently. The way I imagined it was that we were all standing a little closer to the Capitol, I was on a much bigger platform, the guy in the long gown wasn't [George Washington University] President Trachtenberg, but Chief Justice Rehnquist, and my speech began with the words, 'I, Bob Dole . . .'"

★ ★ ★

Theodore Roosevelt once opined, "You don't live there [in the White House]. You are only Exhibit A to the country."

☆

People who visited the White House habitually took White House matchbooks as souvenirs. Franklin Roosevelt decided to solve this problem by imprinting on the matchbooks: "Stolen from the White House."

☆

Truman referred to the White House as "the finest prison in the world."

☆

While instructing her secretary upon settling into the White House in 1961, Jacqueline Kennedy said, "The one thing I do not want to be called is First Lady. It sounds like a saddle horse."

☆

JFK's press secretary, the irrepressible Pierre Salinger, had to face the press when young Caroline Kennedy's pet hamsters escaped in the White House. Salinger announced, "Our security is very tight, but these were extremely intelligent hamsters."

☆

Here's a diary entry by Jimmy Carter: "We had the first of a very relaxed and informal series of meals with our family. Earlier, when Rosalynn was visiting the White House, some of our staff asked the chef and cooks if they thought they could prepare the kind of meals which we enjoyed in the South, and the cook said, 'Yes, ma'am, we've been fixing that kind of food for the servants for a long time!' "

All in the Family

———————— ★ ————————

FOR YEARS JOURNALISTS have portrayed Elizabeth and me as the only two attorneys in Washington, D.C., who trust each other. Even now, some people seem astonished that I am so comfortable sharing the spotlight with a powerful woman. I'm just glad she lets me share it. Back in 1985, when Elizabeth was appointed Secretary of Transportation by President Reagan, her selection inspired a raft of stories. *People* magazine sent a photographer to follow us around for several days. He took about three hundred pictures, of which the magazine wound up using three. One of these showed us making the bed in our Watergate apartment. Shortly after, I got a letter from an irate Californian whose wife had seen the story.

"Senator," he told me, "I don't mind your wife getting a job. I'm sure she is well qualified. She is doing good work. But you've got to stop doing the work around the house. You're causing problems for men all across the country."

"You don't know the half of it," I wrote him back. "The only reason she was helping was because they were taking pictures."

At Elizabeth's Senate confirmation hearing, I paraphrased the great Revolutionary War patriot Nathan Hale, declaring, "I only regret that I have but one wife to give for my country's infrastructure." Elizabeth got me back by asserting her unique qualifications to pass judgment on automobile air bags—after all, she said, she had been driving around with one for years. Since becoming president of the American Red Cross, Elizabeth has provided me with a steady stream of good material. Speaking to the 1993 Gridiron Dinner, just a few months after President Clinton took office, I acknowledged that, whatever our other differences, both the President and I had married determined women. Only with me it was worse: waking up in the morning, I can only wonder how many pints of blood I gave during the night.

Since then, political fund-raising scandals have led me to reassure audiences that they're lucky to have me rather than my wife, because if Elizabeth was on hand she would be after their money *and* their blood.

☆ ☆ ☆

Theodore Roosevelt was once in conference at the White House with the Attorney General, when his young son Quentin Roosevelt came tearing into the room to put three snakes in his father's lap. Roosevelt looked placidly at his son and said, "Hadn't you better go into the next room? Some congressmen are waiting there and the snakes might enliven their tedium."

☆

It was another of Roosevelt's sons who characterized his father thusly: "Father always had to be the center of attention. When he went to a wedding, he wanted to be the bridegroom. And when he went to a funeral, he wanted to be the corpse."

☆

On the day his father became President upon the death of Warren Harding, young Calvin Coolidge, Jr., reported for work as usual in Connecticut Valley tobacco country. An astonished co-worker said, "If my father was President I would not be working in a tobacco field."

To which young Cal answered, "If my father were your father, you would."

☆

Grace Coolidge was one of the most popular of American First Ladies, as warm and outgoing as her husband was taciturn and reserved. In the days before her marriage, Grace had worked at a school for the deaf in western Massachusetts. This prompted Washington wits to say that having taught the deaf to hear, she might teach the dumb to speak.

☆

During the early years of their marriage, Mrs. Coolidge tried a new recipe for apple pie. Unfortunately, it didn't work very well. Coolidge turned to a dinner guest and said, "Don't you think the Road Commissioner would be willing to pay my wife something for her recipe for pie crust?"

☆

When word came that Herbert Hoover had a new granddaughter, he remarked, "Thank God she doesn't have to be confirmed by the Senate."

☆

Eleanor Roosevelt once left the White House to visit a prison in Baltimore. Her departure was so early in the morning that she decided not to disturb her husband. Shortly after he got up, he contacted Mrs. Roosevelt's secretary to ask where his wife was. She replied, "She's in prison, Mr. President."

"I'm not surprised," replied FDR, "but what for?"

☆

Eleanor Roosevelt once gave these tongue-in-cheek instructions: "Campaign behavior for wives: Always be on time. Do as little talking as humanly possible. Lean back in the parade car so everybody can see the President."

☆

After leaving the White House, Harry Truman one morning entered the living room of his home in Independence, Missouri, to discover his wife, Bess, tossing their old love letters into the fireplace. "Think of history!" said a horrified Mr. Truman.

"I have, Harry, I have," said Bess.

Harry Truman made no secret of his disdain for young John F. Kennedy as a prospective Democratic candidate for President in 1960. His opposition had little to do with Kennedy's religion, but much to do with his controversial father. As Truman expressed it: "It's not the Pope I fear but the Pop."

☆

As difficult as it may be to believe today, during the 1960 campaign the American public had trouble differentiating between Robert and John Kennedy. On a flight from Boston to Washington, JFK was seated next to a woman who asked, "Aren't you afraid those terrible labor union racketeers will do something to your seven lovely children?"

Kennedy replied, "That's not me, that's my brother."

As the plane landed, the woman said, "I hope your brother gets to be President."

"That's not my brother," Kennedy rejoined. "That's me."

☆

Robert Kennedy's daughter Kerry once impetuously embraced her father and kissed him vigorously on the cheek. Bobby admonished her, laughing, "Please, Kerry, I told you—only when there are cameramen around."

☆

Hospitalized after an airplane crash in 1964, Ted Kennedy was visited by his brother Robert. A photographer arranging the two for a picture said to Ted, "Move over, you're in your brother's shadow." He replied, "That's the way it will be when we're in the Senate."

☆

After reading a complimentary article about himself, Lyndon Johnson said, "I wish my mother and father could read this. My father would enjoy it and my mother would believe it."

☆

Lynda Bird Johnson told this anecdote about her mother, Lady Bird. "One day, when Mother was shopping in a department store in Austin, she saw a lady who had worked very hard for years in my father's campaigns—she was a real party worker. Mother was in a great hurry and kept arguing with herself—should she take the time to go over and speak or should she just pretend she didn't see her? Of course, she finally went over and gave the lady a big hello. Well, the lady looked straight at Mother for a minute and then asked, 'Do I know you, dearie?' "

☆

Richard Nixon explained his spiritual heritage in one of his 1960 campaign speeches: "My father was a Methodist, my mother was a Quaker. They got married and compromised and my father became a Quaker, too."

☆

As First Lady, Betty Ford charmed America with her openness and honesty. In a speech to members of the Washington, D.C., media years after leaving the White House, she said, "You've heard me say many times that what makes Jerry happy makes me happy. And if you all believe that, you're indeed unsuited for your profession."

Betty Ford once said, "I wish I'd married a plumber. At least he'd be home by five o'clock."

☆

At a political rally, Jimmy Carter once explained why there was such a vast age difference between his three grown sons and his youngest child, Amy: "My wife and I had an argument for fourteen years . . . which I finally won."

☆

Prior to the November 1976 election won by her husband, Rosalynn Carter was asked what Jimmy

Carter had that Gerald Ford did not. "He has me," she replied.

"Don't worry about polls, but if you do, don't admit it."

—ROSALYNN CARTER

☆

During his presidency, Jimmy Carter was not above needling his brother Billy. "I've tried to involve Billy in the government," he once explained. "I was going to put the CIA and the FBI together, but Billy said he wouldn't head an agency that he couldn't spell."

About his somewhat outrageous brother Billy: "A lot of people criticize Billy. But his standing in the public opinion polls is substantially above my own."

☆

Her complete lack of pretense contributed to Barbara Bush's enormous popularity. Referring to her famous faux pearls and gray hair, Mrs. Bush once mocked her own appearance, telling a reporter for *Ladies' Home Journal,* "There is a myth around I don't dress well. I dress very well—I just don't look so good."

In 1990, Barbara Bush addressed the graduating class of Wellesley College, and said, "Somewhere out in this audience may even be someone who will one day follow in my footsteps and preside over the White House as the President's spouse. I wish him well."

☆

Ronald Reagan readily admitted that he owed much of his success in life to his beloved wife, Nancy. Actor Jimmy Stewart, a longtime Reagan friend, put it this way: "If Nancy Reagan instead of Jane Wyman had been Ronald Reagan's first wife, he would never have gone into politics. Instead, she would have seen to it that he got all the best parts, he would have won three or four Oscars, and would have been a real star."

☆

When Nancy Reagan was visiting a school, a student asked her how she liked being married to the President. "Fine," she said, "as long as the President is Ronald Reagan."

The Media

───── ☆ ─────

A S   L O N G   A S there have been politicians, they have been complaining about media bias. Thomas Jefferson is justifiably celebrated as a champion of free speech. Schoolchildren are taught his witticism that, forced to choose between a government without newspapers or newspapers without a government, he would readily opt for the latter. But, as is so often the case with modern journalism, that's not the whole story. At one point during his long political career, Jefferson became so angry over press attacks that he suggested that newspapers should be divided into four sections: (1) Truth, (2) Probability, (3) Possibility, (4) Lies.

Lyndon Johnson took a somewhat more direct approach to the media. *Time*'s distinguished White House correspondent Hugh Sidey recalls his first encounter with the towering Texan. Johnson strolled up to Sidey, put his huge face close to that of the startled journalist, and barked out, "Every reporter I ever met has a character flaw. What's yours?"

It's no secret that I, too, have had a quarrel or two with the press. I remain convinced that many in the press do have a liberal bias, and that facts sometimes lose out to opinion. The fact is that the American economy was prospering in the last year of the Bush administration, but the media told the public day in and day out that we were in either a recession or a depression. President Bush latter summed it all up when he said, "When the Berlin Wall fell, I half expected to see a headline: 'Wall Falls, Three Border Guards Lose Jobs.'"

By and large, however, the majority of reporters I know do their job, and they do it well. And so I meant it in my farewell address to the Senate, when I looked up to the press gallery and said to them, "I don't want [you] to fall out of your seats in shock . . . but I think it's fair to say that while I do not always agree with everything you say or write, I know that what you do off this floor is as vital to American democracy as what we do on it." Come to think of it, however, maybe had one or two of them fallen out of the gallery in shock, they would have been more sympathetic when I fell off that stage in Chico.

Ronald Reagan got it right when he said, "The press can take care of itself quite nicely. And a President should be able to take care of himself as well.

So, what I hope my epitaph will be with the White House correspondents, what every President's epitaph should be with the press is this: He gave as good as he got." So if there are any reporters out there who may be writing my epitaph in thirty or forty years, you can feel free to apply that line to me. And please remember that I want Strom Thurmond to deliver a eulogy at my funeral.

☆ ☆ ☆

There are few more savvy observers of the political scene than David Brinkley. He calls them like he sees them, and minces no words—as can be seen in his observation that "Washington, D.C., is a city filled with people who believe they are important."

☆

William Howard Taft reassured a supporter in 1909, "Don't worry over what the newspapers say. I don't. Why should anyone else? I told the truth to the newspaper correspondents—but when you tell the truth to them they are at sea."

☆

There are so many stories told about "Silent Cal" Coolidge, it's hard to know which ones are true and which ones aren't. Either way, one of my favorites is a report that after Coolidge answered "No" to each of a series of questions put to him by a reporter, he concluded the interview by saying, "Now remember, don't quote me."

☆

At a speech given at a Gridiron Dinner in Washington, D.C., in December 1931, Herbert Hoover said, "A revered President long since dead once told me that there was no solution to this relation of the White House to the press; that there would never be a President who could satisfy the press until he was twenty years dead."

☆

During an off-the-record press conference, Franklin Roosevelt told reporters, "Where I am going I cannot tell you. When I am to get back I cannot tell you. And where I am going on my return I don't know. That's a lot of news, and it can't be released until I am ready."

★

In these days when allegations of media bias are so common, it is easy to forget a time when people read newspapers *because* of their bias. Colonel Robert R. McCormick's *Chicago Tribune* is a case in point. McCormick, whom his critics dubbed the greatest mind of the fourteenth century, made no visible effort to restrict his opinions to the editorial page. Suspicious of anything east of Gary, Indiana, the Colonel reserved a special hatred for New York and its inhabitants. "Tom Dewey is not an American," McCormick grumbled in 1944. "He's a New Yorker."

The Colonel was no more favorably disposed toward those Republicans, led by Michigan's owlish Senator Arthur H. Vandenberg, who embraced an internationalist foreign policy. After Vandenberg underwent a road-to-Damascus experience on America's role in the world, he was regularly berated in the pages of the *Tribune.* A sympathetic constituent stopped the senator one day to offer commiserations after a particularly bitter editorial that assailed him as "Benedict Arnold Vandenberg."

"Actually, I think I am making progress with the Colonel," replied the senator. "For years he called me Judas Iscariot."

☆

McCormick loathed Franklin Roosevelt's New Deal. As part of its coverage of its 1936 Democratic National Convention, the *Tribune* ran a headline declaring, "Soviets Meet at Philadelphia." And when the First Lady found herself in a minor traffic altercation, the *Tribune* thought it worthy of a five-column front-page banner: "Revoke Mrs. FDR's Driver's License."

☆

Adlai Stevenson once said, "Accuracy to a newspaper is what virtue is to a lady, except that a newspaper can always print a retraction."

Stevenson also held that "journalists do not live by words alone, although sometimes they have to eat them."

☆

Stevenson offered this definition: "An editor is one who separates the wheat from the chaff and prints the chaff."

☆

Dwight Eisenhower had to admit, "I can think of nothing more boring for the American public than to have to sit in their living rooms for a whole half hour looking at my face on their television screens."

☆

Barry Goldwater had his problems with the media. "I won't say the papers misquote me, but I sometimes wonder where Christianity would be today if some of those reporters had been Matthew, Mark, Luke, and John."

☆

In May 1962, President Kennedy was asked how he felt the press had treated his administration. He replied, "Well, I'm reading more and enjoying it less."

☆

Bill Moyers, who served at Lyndon Johnson's side for many years, has gone on to a successful career as a commentator. That unique background led him to conclude, "There are honest journalists like there are honest politicians. When bought they stay bought."

☆

In the summer of 1976, Carter told reporters on a press bus in Ohio, "You've treated me very well so far." Compared to what? they asked. "To the way you treated Nixon," he replied.

☆

Soon after he was elected governor, Reagan encountered a good deal of hostility in the press. He remarked, "If this has been a honeymoon, then I've been sleeping alone."

☆

The humorist P. J. O'Rourke is a great admirer of Ronald Reagan. He was especially fond of Reagan's comment during the Iran Contra affair, when the President declared, "I have to admit we considered making one final shipment to Iran, but no one could figure out how to get Sam Donaldson in a crate."

★

When Sam Donaldson yelled over the noise of a helicopter on the South Lawn, "What about Walter Mondale's charges?" Ronald Reagan shot back, "He ought to pay them."

At the Gridiron Dinner in 1988, President Reagan told this story about press conferences, at which he had been known to make some mistakes: "As you know, historians trace the presidential press conference back to a chief executive who was quite reticent with the press, John Quincy Adams. He didn't hold press conferences. But it seems that every morning before dawn, Adams would hike down to the Potomac, strip off his clothes, and swim.

"And one summer day, a woman of the press, under orders from her editor, followed him. And after he'd plunged into the water, she popped from the bushes, sat on his clothes, and demanded an interview. And she told him that if he tried to wade ashore, she'd scream. So Adams held the first press conference up to his neck in water."

Reagan acknowledged that he knew exactly how Adams felt.

Lou Cannon, the veteran reporter and Reagan biographer, recalls a fellow journalist who asked President Reagan to sign a movie photo from *Bedtime for Bonzo*, the film in which the future President starred alongside a chimpanzee. Reagan readily agreed, writing below his name, "I'm the one with the watch."

★

Gary Hart had an interesting idea: "You know what ought to happen in this country to even things out? Reporters ought to have to run for office. Politicians ought to have to write political stories."

★

Nelson Rockefeller withstood press attacks by keeping this philosophy in mind: "Reading about one's failings in the daily papers is one of the privileges of high office in this free country of ours."

☆

The White House birth of puppies to Millie, George and Barbara Bush's beloved springer spaniel (and best-selling author), led President Bush to gloat, "The puppies are sleeping on the *Washington Post* and *New York Times*. It's the first time in history these papers have been used to prevent leaks."

☆

Shortly after he assumed office, Bill Clinton had lunch with the publisher of the *New York Times,* Arthur Sulzberger, Jr. Clinton asked if he had a friend at the *Times.* Sulzberger told him, "The best way of describing our relationship with you is 'tough love.'"

Clinton laughed, and said, "Well, just don't forget the love part."

☆

When asked about the best advice he'd gotten as President about being President, Clinton said, "Never pick a fight with people who buy ink by the barrel."

☆

Speaker Gingrich at the 1998 Gridiron Dinner: "I'm glad to be here tonight. It's nice to see so many of the reporters who have written such flattering puff pieces about me over the years. A former congressman once told me that 'any press is good press.' He'd clearly never seen my press."

Governing

———— ✪ ————

RICHARD NIXON LIKED to recount a 1971 state visit by Tito, the aging leader of Yugoslavia, and a conversation he had with Tito's wife about the last encounter between her husband and Winston Churchill. In his eighties and out of politics, the former Prime Minister was deeply depressed about the state of the world, and even more unhappy about the personal limitations imposed by his doctors. As Tito quaffed scotch and puffed away on a huge cigar, luxuries now denied to Churchill, the old man said to his visitor, "How do you keep so young?"

Without pausing for an answer, Churchill answered his own question, "I know what it is," he blurted out. "It's power. It's power that keeps a man young."

On the other hand, having to share power when you don't want to may contribute to premature aging. Notwithstanding those who believe that the Constitution contains a clause promoting "the general's welfare," there are good reasons why we enshrine the principle of civilian rule in this country. These were never better demonstrated than during the Truman administration, when the President felt his foreign policymaking prerogatives were being usurped by General Douglas MacArthur. To illustrate his point, Truman told of an earlier dispute over military strategy between Abraham Lincoln and General George B. McClellan. A frustrated Lincoln compared himself to the man who was trying to saddle a horse, only to have the horse repeatedly entangle its own rear hoof in the stirrup. "That does it," said the would-be rider. "If you're getting on, then I'm getting off."

Ever since Franklin Roosevelt's New Deal and John F. Kennedy's New Frontier, it's been assumed that academic excellence is a necessary criterion for successful governance. Speaker Sam Rayburn felt differently. Acknowledging the preponderance of Ivy League pedigrees in the Kennedy White House, Rayburn famously observed that he would feel a lot better if just one of them had run for sheriff.

Every elected official in Washington knows that a talented and loyal staff is key to successful governing, and I was fortunate during my years on Capitol Hill to have a staff second to none. We also tried to keep each other from taking ourselves too seriously. When one staff member was a bit aggressive in telling me what to do, I simply said, "If you're so smart, then how come I'm the senator?"

Jimmy Carter and Bill Clinton both arrived at the White House with no experience in dealing with Congress, and both ensured slow starts by appointing White House staffs with limited background in governing. At the 1993 Gridiron Dinner, I told President Clinton and those assembled that I learned firsthand how young the Clinton staff was when I attended a meeting with the Joint Chiefs of Staff, and George Stephanopoulos asked if he could wear General Colin Powell's hat. I also said that I didn't have a problem with the youthfulness of the Clinton staff. "After all," I said, "Chelsea has to have someone to play with."

★ ★ ★

When Will Hays took Will Rogers to the White House to meet President Harding, Rogers said, "Mr. President, I would like to tell you all the latest political jokes."

"You don't have to, Will," Harding rejoined. "I appointed them."

★

Urged to increase spending on military aviation, the thrifty Calvin Coolidge wondered aloud to his cabinet, "Why can't we just buy one airplane and have all the pilots take turns?"

☆

Late in his career, Coolidge reflected, "Perhaps one of the most important accomplishments of my administration has been minding my own business."

☆

Eugene McCarthy despaired, "The only thing that saves us from the bureaucracy is its inefficiency."

☆

Charles de Gaulle had a mordant wit, rarely displayed in public. The Paris telephone system in the 1960s was anything but efficient, as even presidential aides could attest. Walking into the room as a member of his staff slammed down the receiver and exclaimed, "Death to all fools!," de Gaulle observed, "Ah, what a vast program, my friend."

☆

Richard Nixon liked to tell about a visit to the Oval Office from Golda Meir, Israel's plainspoken Prime Minister, shortly after Nixon had named Henry Kissinger Secretary of State. Nixon observed that both of their countries now had Jewish Foreign Ministers. Mrs. Meir, noting Kissinger's thick German accent, answered, "Yes, but mine speaks English."

☆

Everett Dirksen once offered these words, which I commend to all would-be politicians who want to get something accomplished: "I am a man of fixed and unbending principles, the first of which is to be flexible at all times."

☆

Jimmy Carter was not known for his sense of humor, but he got off a good one during a visit to Egypt, when he was told that the Great Pyramid of Giza took twenty years to build. Said Carter, "I'm surprised that a government organization could do it that quickly."

☆

Ronald Reagan once quipped: "Government is like a baby—an alimentary canal with a big appetite at one end and no sense of responsibility at the other."

In 1967, Reagan said, "One way to make sure crime doesn't pay would be to let the government run it."

Reagan also commented, "Government doesn't solve problems; it subsidizes them."

Reagan went so far as to say, "The nine most terrifying words in the English language are 'I'm from the government and I'm here to help.' "

Governments, Reagan observed, "tend not to solve problems, only rearrange them."

"I've been getting some flak," Reagan cracked, "about ordering the production of the B-1. How did I know it was an airplane? I thought it was a vitamin for the troops."

★

In New York City, where colorful characters can be found on virtually any block, there has never been anyone quite like Fiorello La Guardia. As mayor of the Big Apple, Fiorello had his own highly personal style of answering the mail, tossing letters at his secretary and shouting, "Say yes, say no, throw it away, tell him to go to hell."

★

George Bush commented, "Actually, I do have a vision for the nation, and our goal is a simple one: By the time I leave office, I want every single American to be able to set the clock on his VCR."

★

Speaker Gingrich at the 1998 Gridiron Dinner: "For instance, I admit that I mishandled the Air Force One episode. Maybe shutting down the government was a little overkill. I didn't realize the correct answer until I saw the recent Harrison Ford movie.

"Rather than telling the press my feelings were hurt and closing down the government, I should have that night simply taken over the plane."

The Economy

———————— ☆ ————————

AS SOMEONE WHO grew up during the Great Depression, I learned early in life that while the economy may not always be a laughing matter, a sense of humor was a necessary ingredient to surviving tough times. In 1996, I learned another lesson: If you're running against a President in times of economic prosperity, then you'd also better keep your sense of humor, since you may well get more laughs than votes.

There are some who would say that America's tax system is one big joke, and I know a lot of politicians who would agree. Back in the 1920s, President Warren Harding wrestled with a question of tax policy and admitted, "I don't know what to do or where to turn in this taxation matter. Somewhere there must be a book that tells all about it, where I could go to straighten it out in my mind. But I don't know where the book is, and maybe I couldn't read it if I found it." Half a century later, Louisiana senator Russell

Long, who preceded me as chairman of the Senate Finance Committee, proved that the more things change, the more they stay the same. As he guided the 1978 tax bill through the Finance Committee, a junior senator asked for an explanation of a pending vote. "If everyone knew what they were voting on," Long cracked, "we'd never get out of here."

Will Rogers used to say that the American tax code produced more liars than anything but golf. All joking aside, I confess that I've searched the Constitution, and I can't find any amendment that requires the complex and confusing tax code inflicted upon us. In fact, now that I'm back at a law firm, maybe I'll take a case arguing that our current tax code is unconstitutional because it is "cruel and unusual punishment."

Ronald Reagan once told a Gridiron Dinner audience, "I am not worried about the deficit. It is big enough to take care of itself." While mortgaging the future of our children should not be a joking matter, I confess that, like Reagan, I did occasionally take the opportunity to find the light side in the budget deficit. One story—and you can decide whether it's true or not—that I often repeated involved the 1995 Senate debate on the proposed Balanced Budget Amendment. During the debate, Senator Robert Byrd, who is a master of Roman history, rose and said, "If Cicero was alive today, he would oppose the Balanced Budget Amendment." At which point, Senator Strom Thurmond jumped up and said, "I knew Cicero. Cicero was a friend of mine. And I know he was in favor of a Balanced Budget Amendment."

During my first appearance on *The Late Show with David Letterman* in February 1995, I offered my own take on Letterman's famous Top 10 List—the Top 7 Ways to Balance the Budget. (The reason my list had 7 and not 10, I explained, was that Republicans were cutting everything by 30 percent.) My list included: Stop paying Clinton speechwriters by the word; Saving government ink by replacing the long William Jefferson Clinton signature with 66 percent shorter Bob Dole signature; Making Gore and Gingrich pay for those good seats at State of the Union addresses; Firing the White House gardeners and requiring Al Gore to do something to earn his keep. And the No. 1 way to balance the budget? Sell Arkansas.

☆ ☆ ☆

In 1932, three years after Calvin Coolidge had left office, a friend told him, "I wish it was you that we were voting for in November. It would be the end of this horrible depression."

"It would be the beginning of mine," Coolidge replied.

☆

With remarkable prescience, Herbert Hoover once remarked, "Blessed are the young, for they shall inherit the national debt."

☆

Eisenhower and John Foster Dulles were enjoying a cruise on the Potomac aboard the presidential yacht. They found themselves discussing the anecdote about George Washington's ability to throw a silver dollar across the Potomac, from one shore to the other. As the yacht passed the point where Washington was supposed to have performed this toss, Dulles remarked that the distance between shores seemed so great that the story, like several other famous Washington anecdotes, should be regarded as apocryphal. "One thing must be remembered," countered Eisenhower. "A dollar went a great deal further in those days than it does now."

☆

John F. Kennedy explained the economic plight of farmers: "The farmer is the only man in our economy who buys everything at retail, sells everything he produces at wholesale, and pays the freight both ways."

☆

In 1973, Reagan bemoaned the state of the American economy: "Do you remember back in the days when you thought that nothing could replace the dollar? Today it practically has."

In May 1980, while campaigning for the presidency, Reagan chastised his opponent: "Carter said he'd do something about unemployment. He did. In April, 825,000 Americans lost their jobs."

Ronald Reagan is a great storyteller. One of his favorites concerned three men, a surgeon, an engineer, and an economist, who had passed away and eventually confronted St. Peter at the gates of heaven. "I'm very sorry," Peter told them, "but there is room for only one of you. Which one of you is from the oldest profession?"

The surgeon said, "That's me! God took Adam's rib and made Eve, so he was doing surgery."

"No," asserted the engineer. "Before that, God

made the world out of chaos, and that took engineering."

Finally the economist spoke up. "Wait a minute!" he declared. "Who do you think *made* all that chaos?"

The government's view of the economy, said Ronald Reagan, is summed up in just a few short phrases: "If it moves, tax it; if it keeps moving, regulate; if it stops moving, subsidize it."

President Reagan's pollster, Dick Wirthlin, recalls a low point early in 1983, when unemployment was at its peak and the economic boom we now associate with the Reagan presidency had yet to occur. Making no attempt to hide the bad news, Wirthlin told the President that for the first time since he took office, a majority of Americans disapproved of his job performance.

"Dick, I know what we can do," an unconcerned Reagan told Wirthlin. "I will just have to go and get shot again."

☆

On the Senate floor, where things were obviously getting out of hand, Everett Dirksen quipped, "A billion here, a billion there, and pretty soon you're talking about real money."

☆

When Senator Fred Thompson of Tennessee arrived in Washington in 1994 he brought with him a background of acting in a number of movies and a razor wit. Early in his Senate term, he cracked, "I've still got a lot to learn about Washington. Why, yesterday I accidentally spent some of my own money."

☆

Phil Gramm and I have had our occasional differences, but we do share a love for one-liners. One of the times I thought "I wish I had said that" was when Phil said, "Balancing the budget is like going to heaven. Everybody wants to do it, but nobody wants to make the trip."

Religion

─── ☆ ───

PEOPLE DON'T JOKE about religion
these days. Oh sure, the devout Jimmy Carter
was sometimes accused of taking his initials
too seriously. In fact, when Carter attended a National Prayer Breakfast during his presidency, Bishop
Fulton J. Sheen brought down the house with his
opening remarks. "Fellow sinners," he intoned, before turning to President Carter and said, "And that
means you, too." Thankfully, however, stories featuring the proverbial priest, rabbi, and minister have
gone the way of ethnic humor and dialect jokes.

The late Massachusetts congressman Silvio Conte
was a good friend of mine, and his storytelling ability
rivaled that of his best friend, Tip O'Neill. Sil delighted in telling this anecdote—which also made the
point that it is dangerous to mix politics and religion:
"One Sunday I missed church because I was tied up
with constituents, and some people said being down
in Washington had made an atheist out of me. Several

weeks later, when I was back home again and did get to church, they said, 'Why, that pious fraud, he's just trying to dig up votes!' "

One of the great traditions of American politics is the Al Smith Dinner, sponsored each year by the Catholic Diocese of New York. In 1993, Cardinal John O'Connor asked me to serve as keynote speaker. Every officeholder and office seeker in New York politics was there—including Mayor David Dinkins and his Republican opponent, Rudy Giuliani. The two men were locked in a close mayoral race, with election day just a week away. Not wanting to inject religion into politics—but wanting to put in a good word for the Republican—I made reference to the fact that Republican Dick Riordan had been elected mayor of Los Angeles earlier in the year. "If a Republican can be elected mayor of Los Angeles and New York City in the same year," I said with more or less a straight face, "then who among us can doubt the existence of miracles?"

☆ ☆ ☆

One Sunday, when Calvin Coolidge returned from church, his wife asked him what the minister had spoken about.

"Sin," said Coolidge.

"What did he say about it?" she asked.

"He was against it."

☆

In the spring of 1929, First Lady Lou Henry Hoover touched off a national controversy by inviting the wife of a black congressman from Chicago to the White House. Amazing as it seems, this was the first time that an African-American woman had ever been received there socially. The gesture did not sit well with some traditionalists, especially in the South. The Texas legislature went so far as to propose impeaching the President. Mrs. Hoover apologized to her husband for adding to his troubles.

"Don't worry, Lou," said the President. "One of the consolations of orthodox religion is that it provides a hot hell for the Texas legislator."

☆

Asked about his churchgoing, FDR replied, "I can do almost anything in the goldfish bowl, but I'll be hanged if I can say my prayers in it."

☆

When Edward Everett Hale served as chaplain of the Senate, he was asked, "Do you pray for the senators, Dr. Hale?"

"No," he said. "I look at the senators and pray for the country."

☆

During the 1952 campaign, Adlai Stevenson appeared before a Baptist convention in Houston, at which his host declared, "Governor Stevenson, before I introduce you, I want to make it clear that you are here as a courtesy, because Dr. Norman Vincent Peale has already instructed us to vote for your opponent. Ladies and gentlemen, Governor Stevenson."

Unfazed, Stevenson walked to the microphone and said, "Well, speaking as a Christian, I would like to say that I find the Apostle Paul appealing and the Apostle Peale appalling."

☆

When he was blackballed by an anti-Semitic golf club in Phoenix, Goldwater allegedly remarked, "Since I'm only half Jewish, can I join if I only play nine holes?"

☆

John F. Kennedy employed humor to dispose of the religious issue in the 1960 campaign. "The reporters are constantly asking me my views of the Pope's infallibility," he declared. "And so I asked my friend Cardinal Spellman what I should say when reporters ask me whether I feel the Pope is infallible. And Cardinal Spellman said, 'I don't know what to tell you, Senator. All I know is that he keeps calling me Spillman.' "

☆

During the 1960 campaign, Kennedy was sarcastically asked, "Do you think a Protestant can be elected President in 1960?"

He answered, "If he's prepared to answer how he stands on the issue of the separation of church and state, I see no reason why we should discriminate against him."

In fact, there was some criticism in higher Catholic quarters that Kennedy tried too hard to show that he wasn't influenced by the Vatican. When asked about this, Kennedy told reporters, "Now I understand why Henry VIII set up his own church."

☆

Saying grace before a White House dinner in 1965, press secretary Bill Moyers spoke very softly. "Speak up, Bill!" President Johnson bellowed. "Speak up!"

"I wasn't addressing you, Mr. President," Moyers replied.

☆

Ronald Reagan once remarked, "We are told that God is dead. Well, He isn't. We just can't talk to Him in the classroom anymore."

On the subject of religion, Ronald Reagan liked to quote Ben Franklin's admonition: "Work as if you were to live a hundred years. Pray as if you were to die tomorrow."

☆

At a National Prayer Luncheon, Hillary Clinton once said, "In the Bible it says they asked Jesus how many times you should forgive, and he said seventy times seven. Well, I want you all to know that I'm keeping a chart."

War

— ☆ —

THE WORLD SEEMED to hold its collective breath in the autumn of 1962, when the United States and the Soviet Union nearly went to war over Cuba. At the height of the crisis, President Kennedy secretly dispatched former Secretary of State Dean Acheson to brief French President Charles de Gaulle at the Elysée Palace in Paris. Acheson outlined the tense situation from the American standpoint. He also offered to show the French leader a series of reconnaissance photos which established beyond doubt the presence of Soviet medium-range nuclear missiles on Cuban soil. Under the circumstances, said Acheson, there might be no alternative to war.

"You may tell the President," said de Gaulle, "that if there is a war, France will be with you."

De Gaulle next received the Soviet Ambassador to France, Sergei Vinogradov. "Well, Mr. Ambassador, I am listening," he declared. Vinogradov painted a lurid picture of impending nuclear holocaust. De Gaulle, convinced that his visitor was bluffing, remained silent as the Soviet diplomat described ever more horrible calamities. When he was through, de Gaulle rose and stretched out his hand in farewell. "At least, Mr. Ambassador, we'll die together!" he said to Vinogradov. "Goodbye, Mr. Ambassador."

☆ ☆ ☆

Theodore Roosevelt bitterly resented Woodrow Wilson's refusal to permit him to recruit a volunteer division to fight in World War I. Getting in a dig at Wilson's famed, if unkept, campaign promise from 1916, TR declared, "I am the only one he has kept out of war."

☆

Asked to explain why he had not fought in Europe during World War I, Huey P. Long did not mince words. "I did not go," said Huey, "because I was not mad at anyone over there."

☆

Winston Churchill remarked, "Nothing in life is so exhilarating as to be shot at without result."

Churchill said to an impatient Franklin Roosevelt on the projected duration of the Yalta Conference with Stalin, "I do not see any other way of realizing our hopes about a World Organization in five or six days. Even the Almighty took seven."

☆

The great comedian Will Rogers gave voice to widespread doubts concerning America's diplomatic performance. "The United States has never lost a war or won a conference," he declared. Rogers also claimed to be clairvoyant on the subject of future wars. "If you want to know when a war might be coming," he told audiences, "you just watch the United States and see when it starts cutting down on its defenses. It's the surest barometer in the world."

☆

When he was British Resident Minister in Algeria during World War II, Harold Macmillan was asked to settle a dispute between American and British officers in the Allied mess. It seems Americans wanted drinks served before dinner, and the British after. Macmillan's solution: "Henceforth, we will all drink before meals in deference to the Americans and we will all drink after in deference to the British."

☆

In January 1966, Republican senator George Aiken of Vermont, discussing the war in Vietnam, said, "I'm not very keen for doves or hawks. I think we need more owls."

☆

In 1970, Ronald Reagan observed, "To blame the military for war makes about as much sense as suggesting that we get rid of cancer by getting rid of doctors."

Off Hours

—————— ⭐ ——————

NOTHING IS AS GOOD for the inside of a man as the outside of a horse," proclaimed Ronald Reagan, who often escaped the pressures of the presidency by traveling to his beloved California ranch. Reagan, like Presidents before and since, also took time to exchange the challenges of the Oval Office for those of the golf course. Even when he was talking about golf, however, Reagan never strayed far from his political message. He once joked that when comedian Bob Hope asked him what his handicap was, his response was "The Congress."

No President loved golf more than Dwight Eisenhower. Ike loved to tell the story of inviting a friend to join his foursome one day only to have the man say that he had promised his wife he would do something else. "Tell her you've changed your mind," Eisenhower urged his friend. "After all, are you a man or a mouse?" "I'm a man," his friend replied. "My wife is afraid of a mouse." After leaving the White House, Eisenhower was asked if there was a difference in his golf game. "Yes," he replied. "I lose a lot more now."

Jerry Ford also had more time for golf after leaving the White House, but if the comedians are to be believed, it didn't improve his game. His errant drives led Bob Hope to quip that "President Ford waits until he hits his first drive to know what course he's playing that day." Ford also delighted in Hope's quip that "President Ford had a good day on the golf course. He got an eagle, a birdie, a moose, an elk, and two Masons."

President Clinton is a golfer, as well, but early in his presidency he was better known for his love of jogging. In fact, soon after he took office, I made a contribution to a fund established for the purpose of building a jogging track on the White House grounds. I explained my gesture at the 1993 Gridiron Dinner by saying, "I would rather have the President running around down there than running around on Capitol Hill."

My war injuries have always prevented me from playing golf, but even if they hadn't, I don't know if I would like the game. After all, how could a proponent of a balanced budget enjoy a sport where you go for the green, only to end up in the hole?

Instead, Elizabeth and I both spend time each day on our treadmill. It's a perfect piece of exercise equipment for someone used to legislative battles on Capitol

Hill. You go for hours and hours, but you always stay in the same place. And ever since Elizabeth presented him to me upon my election as Senate Republican leader in 1984, we have taken great joy in our miniature schnauzer, Leader. One of the most well-attended press conferences I've ever seen was the one in 1990 when Elizabeth and I joined Senator Thurmond in displaying Leader, Chelsea (Senator Thurmond's schnauzer), and a litter of their puppies. Elizabeth commented that puppies were Democrats when they were born, but became Republicans when they opened their eyes. And I took joy in describing how they were being paper-trained with the *New York Times.*

☆ ☆ ☆

Mrs. Coolidge liked to tell this story about her husband. When he was Vice President, a dinner companion said to him, "You must talk to me, Mr. Coolidge. I made a bet today that I could get more than two words out of you."

"You lose," said Coolidge.

As Vice President, Coolidge was invited to many dinners. He was always the despair of his various hostesses because he had complete disregard for the art of conversation. One woman felt she had solved this problem by seating him next to Alice Roosevelt Longworth, a widely celebrated conversationalist.

Longworth began to chat in her usual enchanting manner, but was unable to get any response from Coolidge. Finally, in utter exasperation, she asked pointedly, "You go to so many dinners. They must bore you a great deal."

Coolidge replied without lifting his eyes from the plate before him. "Well, a man has to eat somewhere."

☆

There were two things no man should be forced to do in public, Hoover liked to say. One was pray; the other was fish. So he wrote a book on fishing, extolling its democratic joys, "for all men are equal before fishes."

☆

During a rather heated argument, Lady Astor said in exasperation to Churchill, "If you were my husband, I'd poison your coffee."

Churchill replied, "If you were my wife, I'd drink it."

⭐

On the legendary—and very crowded—Inaugural Balls, held on January 20, 1961, JFK quipped, "The Johnsons and I have been to five balls tonight, and we still have one unfulfilled ambition—and that is to see somebody dance."

⭐

William Howard Taft was a great jurist and a very capable administrator, but he was no politician. During Taft's 1908 run for the presidency, Republican strategists feared a voter backlash when it was revealed their candidate was a Unitarian. Taft compounded the problem by insisting on playing golf on the Sabbath. His political patron, Theodore Roosevelt, fairly begged Taft to stay off the links—at least until after election day.

Taft, ever the legalist, professed to be confused. "But, Theodore," he said, "you play tennis," a game then regarded as even more elitist than golf.

"But there is a difference, Will," replied TR. "I don't let them take my picture."

✯

Once asked what he did for exercise, Calvin Coolidge replied, "Having my picture taken."

✯

Wilson's definition of golf is a classic. It was, he said, "an ineffectual attempt to put an elusive ball into an obscure hole with implements ill adapted to the purpose."

✯

Teddy Roosevelt's daughter Alice Roosevelt Longworth told the tale of the merchant seaman who was being interrogated under the provisions of the Mc-Carran Act. The investigator asked, "Do you have any pornographic literature?"

"Pornographic literature!" the seaman exclaimed indignantly. "I don't even have a pornograph!"

✯

Churchill's appreciation of liquor was widely known. On one occasion, he was scheduled to make a speech before a small gathering. The chairman introduced him by saying, "If all the spirits consumed by Sir Winston were poured into this room, it would reach up to here on the wall." And with that, he drew a line on the wall with his finger at about eye level.

Churchill got up to speak. Studying the imaginary line on the wall, he looked up at the ceiling and made a mathematical calculation with his fingers. Heaving a sigh, he said, "Ah, so much to be done, and so little time in which to do it."

Further Churchill remarks on the subject of alcohol: "Most people hate the taste of beer—to begin with. It is, however, a prejudice that many people have been able to overcome."

At a party in the House of Commons one evening, a socialist member of the House from Liverpool, Miss Bessie Braddock, told Churchill, "Winston, you're drunk."

Churchill instantly retorted, "Bessie, you're ugly, and tomorrow morning I'll be sober, but you'll still be ugly."

☆

Churchill recalled, "When I was a young subaltern in the South African war, the water was not fit to drink. To make it palatable, we had to add whiskey. By diligent effort, I learned to like it."

Churchill quipped, "I have taken more out of alcohol than alcohol has taken out of me."

Encountering Attlee in the men's room of the House of Commons one day, the Prime Minister distanced himself as far as possible from his socialist rival. "Feeling standoffish today, are we, Winston?" asked Attlee.

"That's right," said Churchill. "Every time you see something big, you want to nationalize it."

☆

On a bet, Barry Goldwater taught himself to play a fairly recognizable version of "Silent Night" on the trombone. But when it came to the bagpipe: "I can't figure out how to hold the doggone thing. It's like making love to an octopus."

☆

When Johnson was asked by a reporter what his golf handicap was, he quipped, "I don't have any handicap. I am all handicap."

☆

During the 1960 campaign, a reporter asked Nixon what kind of vacation he planned after the election, noting that he had never seen Nixon play golf. Nixon replied, "Your comment . . . is probably the most objective comment about the quality of my golf that I've ever heard."

☆

"The three-martini lunch is the epitome of American efficiency. Where else can you get an earful, a bellyful, and a snootful at the same time?"

—GERALD FORD

☆

Kennedy and Johnson Administration Agriculture Secretary Orville Freeman often told outdoor groups, "The Lord created the world two-thirds water and one-third land, with the obvious intention that man should spend two-thirds of his time fishing and one-third working."

☆

When Walter Mondale was appointed Ambassador to Japan he quickly decided that the best part of his job was this: "When Washington was awake, I am asleep. And even better, when I am awake, Washington is sleeping."

☆

Ribbing Bob Hope, Reagan told an audience gathered for a Hope celebration, "He's entertained six Presidents. He's performed for twelve."

☆

When he announced he would not run again for the Senate, then Majority Leader George Mitchell was rumored to be interested in the position of Commissioner of Major League Baseball. When he was asked if he could deal with the monumental egos of the twenty-eight owners of major league teams, Mitchell said, "In my case that would be a 72 percent reduction."

☆

In her memoirs, Barbara Bush described one of those most embarrassing moments that inevitably occur, even on the most carefully advanced of foreign trips. Along with her husband, then the Vice President, Mrs. Bush was lunching with Emperor Hirohito at Tokyo's Imperial Palace. Sitting next to the Emperor, Mrs. Bush found the conversation an uphill task. To all her efforts at verbal engagement, the Emperor would smile and say "Yes" or "No," with an occasional "Thank you" tossed in for good measure. Looking around her elegant surroundings, she complimented Hirohito on his official residence.

"Thank you," he said.

"Is it new?" pressed Mrs. Bush.

"Yes."

"Was the old palace just so old that it was falling down?" asked the intrepid visitor.

In his most charming, yet regal, manner, Hirohito replied, "No, I'm afraid that you bombed it."

Mrs. Bush turned to her other lunch partner.

★

Commenting in January 1996 on the TV show *The Simpsons,* which portrayed President and Mrs. Bush in an episode, President Bush said, "It was fine. The only thing missing was Oliver Stone as the director."

★

On his invitation to former Japanese Prime Minister Kiichi Miyazawa to attend a Bush Presidential Library function, President Bush quipped, "Some of you may remember him as the Japanese Prime Minister I threw up on." I told him, "This time, the dinner's on me."

★

On why he chose to learn to play the saxophone, Bill Clinton said, in reference to a certain other famous remark, "You don't have to inhale. You blow out."

Politics as Usual

───────────── ✦ ─────────────

MY WHOLE FAMILY were Democrats," Ronald Reagan once said. "As a matter of fact, I had an uncle who won a medal once for never having missed voting in an election for fifteen years . . . and he's been dead for fourteen."

Reagan was joking, but many Americans probably view the political arena as a place where elections are rigged, where lobbyists move from senator to senator passing out sacks of cash, and where there is a personal motive behind every public action.

To be sure, there are dishonest politicians, just as there are dishonest folks in any occupation. But I learned in my thirty-five years on Capitol Hill that the overwhelming majority of men and women in the political arena were honest people who were motivated not by the chance to make a lot of money (which you don't in public service), but by the chance to make a difference for their community, state, and nation.

And perhaps one of the reasons that I joked so

much is that I wanted to send a message that politics can be fun, and it is a field that is open to everyone. After all, if the two nominees for the highest office in the land hail from Russell, Kansas, and Hope, Arkansas, then there is no limit to what can be accomplished.

Throughout my career, I have battled against the "politics as usual" perception by trying to open doors long closed to women, to minorities, and to those with disabilities. I have also done what I can to ensure that the highest levels of government were not reserved to those with Ivy League pedigrees.

When the Reagan administration was putting together its cabinet, I watched as all the plum positions were handed out to Wall Street bankers, Washington, D.C., insiders, and California friends of President Reagan. I was promoting a well-regarded Illinois farmer named John Block for Secretary of Agriculture, and I took it upon myself to administer a little geography lesson to the Reagan team. I got a map of the United States and drew a big red circle around the middle. I sent the map to my senatorial colleague Paul Laxalt, a Reagan intimate who was heavily involved in personnel matters. "Paul," I wrote in an accompanying note, "that blank space is what is referred to as the Midwest."

A few days later, John Block got the appointment.

* * *

Theodore Roosevelt once remarked, "I took the Canal Zone and let Congress debate, and while the debate goes on, the canal does, too."

*

On one occasion, Woodrow Wilson confronted a political hack whose ambition for a judicial appointment led him to lobby the governor furiously. What began as a polite conversation soon turned into an argument, with both men raising their voices. Wilson refused to compromise with his own high standards. The outraged office seeker put on his hat and angrily stamped out of the room, shouting as he went, "Mr. Wilson, you're no gentleman!"

"And, Mr. Smith," said Wilson, "you're no judge!"

*

Few American Presidents have been so controversial as FDR. Even members of his own party in Congress resented the President's habit of reserving power to himself. Near the end of one especially bitter gripe session, Senator Henry Ashurst of Arizona tried to put things in perspective. "After all," said Ashurst, "Roosevelt is his own worst enemy."

"Not while I'm alive, he ain't," rejoined Senator Cotton Ed Smith of South Carolina.

☆

Huey Long, a strong Roosevelt supporter in 1932, soon turned against the father of the New Deal, and harbored dreams of winning the White House for himself in 1936. Long angered other Democrats by suggesting there wasn't a dime's worth of difference between FDR and his Republican predecessor.

"Hoover is a hoot owl. Roosevelt is a scrooch owl," said Huey. "A hoot owl bangs in the nest and knocks the hen clean out and catches her while she is falling. The scrooch owl slips into the roost and scrooches up to the hen and talks softly to her. And the first thing you know—there ain't no hen."

☆

In a speech to the House of Commons in January 1941, Churchill insisted, "I do not at all resent criticism, even when, for the sake of emphasis, it for a time parts company with reality."

In 1947, Churchill, then leader of the loyal opposition, made this remark to the House of Commons: "When I am abroad, I always make it a rule never to criticize or attack the government of my own country. I make up for lost time when I come home."

Churchill made no attempt to conceal his ego, which was as outsized as his achievements. Following a heated dispute Churchill upbraided his valet, "You were rude," said Churchill.

"You were rude, too," replied the manservant.

"But I am a great man," said Churchill. End of argument.

Churchill enjoyed needling Clement Attlee, leader of the opposition Labour party. He once described Attlee as "a modest man with much to be modest about."

☆

Shortly after Hitler came into power, efforts were made to obtain a visa to enable a famous German author to come to the United States so that he would not be put in a concentration camp. A request was made directly to FDR, who agreed.

But days passed and nothing happened, and Roosevelt was asked about it again. Once more he put through the request, saying, "You know, I hope before this thing is over, the State Department will be on our side."

☆

Harry Truman recalled, "During one of my first sessions in the Senate, J. Hamilton Lewis came over and sat down by me. He was from Illinois and was the whip in the Senate at that time. 'Don't start out with an inferiority complex,' he told me. 'For the first six months, you'll wonder how you got here—after that you'll wonder how the rest of us got here.' "

☆

Truman made this famous remark, which has often been repeated over the years: "If you want a friend in Washington, get a dog."

⭐

Senator Norris Cotton of New Hampshire once made this insightful contrast between the two chambers of the legislature: "The House maintains a barbershop, where congressmen pay fifty cents for a haircut, but custom dictates that they tip an additional fifty cents, so it costs them a dollar. The Senate is different. You get the haircut free, but the traditional tip is a dollar. So, you see, the haircut is as free as most things furnished by the government."

Senator Cotton also made this observation about a particularly frugal, budget-conscious Congress: "The boys are in such a mood that if someone introduced the Ten Commandments, they'd cut them down to eight."

⭐

 ${\rm A}$ dlai Stevenson offered the following definition: "An independent is someone who wants to take the politics out of politics."

☆

 ${\rm W}$ hen John Gardner assumed the duties of Secretary of Health, Education, and Welfare, he was filled with optimism: "We are all faced with a series of great opportunities—brilliantly disguised as insoluble problems."

☆

 ${\rm J}$ ohn F. Kennedy made light of political fund-raising when he addressed one of several-hundred-dollars-a-plate dinners in the fall of 1960. "I am deeply touched," he told one such audience in Salt Lake City. "Not as deeply touched as you have been by coming to this dinner; nevertheless, it is a sentimental occasion."

 ${\rm K}$ ennedy once said, "My experience in government is that when things are noncontroversial, beautifully coordinated, and all the rest, it must be that there is not much going on."

☆

At a bill-signing ceremony in the White House in December 1963, Lyndon Johnson said, as he handed one of the pens he had used to Speaker John McCormack, "I found out that if you get along with the Speaker, you get these signing ceremonies more often. I think the Speaker works on the basis that a bill a day keeps the President away."

President Johnson liked to tell a story that illustrated his feelings about the vast number of consultants that had proliferated in Washington over the years. According to LBJ, there was a bulldog back home in Johnson City that made all the female dogs in town pregnant every spring. Eventually the local ladies got so fed up that they banded together and had the bulldog fixed. You can imagine their surprise the next spring when all the female dogs were again pregnant.

"It's that damned old bulldog again," said one of the ladies.

"But didn't we have him fixed?" asked another.

"We did," replied the first lady. "But now he's acting as a consultant."

☆

Leave it to the inimitable Alice Roosevelt Longworth to offer the ultimate insider's assessment of scandals surrounding the Nixon Administration. In the words of Princess Alice, "I will remember Watergate as good, unclean fun."

☆

Eugene McCarthy noted, "Being in politics is like being a football coach. You have to be smart enough to understand the game . . . and dumb enough to think it's important."

☆

Few people know Washington, D.C., better than former Nixon White House aide and longtime lobbyist Tom Korologos. Tom has guided many a presidential appointee through the confirmation process, which led him to say, "Washington is like Salem. If we're not lynching somebody twenty-four hours a day in this wretched town, we're not happy."

☆

Korologos also said, "The things Congress does best are nothing and overreacting."

☆

Gerald Ford once declared, "A bronco is something that kicks and bucks, twists and turns, and very seldom goes in one direction. We have one of those things here in Washington—it's called the Congress."

☆

When it comes to debating budget appropriations, congressmen naturally guard their own projects jealously, but slice cheerfully away at their colleagues' recommendations. Mo Udall liked to tell this illustrative story: "Hanging his coat on a restaurant rack, a man sat down to dine. A thief seized his coat, put it on, and began to run away. The coat's owner, enlisting a nearby policeman, gave chase. The officer ordered the thief to halt; when he kept on running, the coat's owner shouted, 'Shoot him in the pants!' "

★

House Speaker Tip O'Neill quipped, "I'm against any deal I'm not in on."

★

Former Secretary of State Al Haig often had his own unique way with the English language. "That's not a lie," he once said. "It's a terminological inexactitude."

★

Ronald Reagan quipped, "Politics is just like show business. You need a big opening. Then you coast for a while. Then you need a big finish."

In the aftermath of the assassination attempt of 1981, soon after Reagan regained consciousness, his aide Lyn Nofziger reported to him, "You'll be happy to know that the government is running normally."

Reagan replied without hesitation, "What makes you think I'd be happy about that?"

☆

Margaret Thatcher once said, "I always cheer up immensely if an attack is particularly wounding, because I think, well, if they attack me personally, it means they have not a single political argument left."

☆

George magazine published a story strongly implying that John Travolta, a dedicated Scientologist, had toned down the less flattering aspects of his portrayal in the movie *Primary Colors* because Clinton had promised to do what he could to help end discrimination against Scientologists in the Soviet Union. At the 1998 Gridiron Dinner, in connection with Travolta's performance, Clinton deadpanned, "I'm pleased to announce the National Museum of Scientology will be opening soon on the Mall."

Free Advice

———— ☆ ————

POLITICAL ADVICE IS a bit like your average Christmas fruitcake: something everyone gives and nobody wants. Running for President, you get more advice than votes. For my money, the best political counsel I ever received came from my Senate predecessor, Frank Carlson, a shrewd student of human nature who understood that individual voters don't always think, much less vote, like the organizations that presume to speak for them. Frank once received two telephone calls within an hour from the same Chamber of Commerce back home in Kansas. The first was a demand for economy in government; the second insisted that Carlson obtain a federally funded water project to benefit farmers. Illogical? Sure. But that's politics.

A very different adviser was Nelson Rockefeller, who offered some friendly guidance in the course of a swing across upstate New York during the 1976 campaign. I was taking a pounding in the national press, and like most politicians, I wasn't inclined to suffer in silence. A sympathetic Rockefeller pulled me over to one side. "I never read anything about myself in the papers," he said. "My advice to you is to do the same. Otherwise you'll spend half the day reading the criticism and the other half reacting."

Only later did I wonder whether this advice had anything to do with his name. For millions of Americans of a certain age, "rich as Rockefeller" conjured up an image very different from being on the dole. Come to think of it, that was the same trip when the Vice President of the United States, obviously vexed by some hecklers, responded by giving them the finger. Now that's self-confidence.

On occasion I have administered some advice of my own. Once in the 1980s I received a letter, addressed to "Bob Dole, Washington, D.C." The outside of the envelope was covered with abusive language, colorfully repeated and expanded upon inside. I wasn't sure at first how to respond. I didn't want to insult my secretary by giving it to her to read. On investigation, the letter turned out to be from a Kansas banker, who was decidedly unhappy with me over some legislation I had sponsored at the request of the Reagan White House (which wasn't any too pleased itself after the bill failed an early test vote). I thought about putting the letter in the *Congressional Record*, figuring no one would ever see it there.

Then I remembered the example of the late Senator Steven Young, a feisty Democrat from Ohio whose reaction upon receiving a similarly abusive letter many years before was part of senatorial legend. In the spirit of Senator Young I drafted a short note to my banker correspondent, which I then attached to his own communication. "Some damn fool sent me this letter and signed your name to it," I wrote.

You know what? I haven't heard from him since.

Another sage bit of advice was recalled by the late Senator Ed Muskie, a marvelous raconteur who liked to tell Coolidge stories. As the retiring governor of Massachusetts, Coolidge was asked by his successor, "How did you manage to see so many visitors in a day and always leave the office at 5 P.M.? I find that I have to stay as late as 9 P.M. What is the difference?"

"You talk back," said Coolidge.

☆ ☆ ☆

"The most successful politician is he who says what everybody is thinking most often and in the loudest voice."

—THEODORE ROOSEVELT

☆

To explain his lifelong terseness, Calvin Coolidge would say, "I have never been hurt by anything I didn't say."

And: "If you don't say anything, you won't be called upon to repeat it."

☆

Theodore Roosevelt made no secret of his contempt for those he called "malefactors of great wealth." Nor was he especially impressed by college graduates. As he put it: "A man that has never gone to school may steal from a freight car, but if he has a university education, he may steal the whole railroad."

☆

Woodrow Wilson wrote to Bernard Baruch in 1916, "I am inclined to follow the course suggested by a friend, who says that he has always followed the rule never to murder a man who is committing suicide."

☆

Before leaving office, Coolidge offered the following advice to incoming President Herbert Hoover.

"You have to put up with three or four hours of visitors every day. Nine-tenths of them want something they ought not to have. If you keep dead still, they will run down in three or four minutes. If you even cough or smile, they will start up all over again."

☆

In the depths of the Great Depression, Hoover and Coolidge found themselves together in Marion, Ohio, dedicating the memorial to Warren G. Harding. Hoover outlined all the steps he was taking to end the nation's economic spiral, making clear his resentment over what he regarded as unfair criticism from the public.

"You can't expect to see calves running in the field the day after you put the bull to the cows," said Coolidge.

"No," replied Hoover, "but I would expect to see contented cows."

When his niece expressed alarm over dinner speakers who overstepped the bounds of their allotted time, Hoover gave her some homely advice. "You just pass them up a little note saying 'Your fly is open' and he'll sit down right away."

★

Told that familiarity breeds contempt, Churchill responded, "I would like to remind you that without a degree of familiarity we could not breed anything."

★

Harry Truman had no illusions about his place in history. "This administration is going to be cussed and discussed for years to come," he said.

Truman once advised, "If you can't convince them, confuse them."

★

Adlai Stevenson declared, "Nothing so dates a man as decrying the younger generation."

☆

Dwight Eisenhower cautioned, "Sweet praise is like perfume. It's fine if you don't swallow it."

☆

In the words of JFK: "Politics is like football. If you see daylight, go through the hole."

Kennedy also warned, "Forgive your enemies, but never forget their names."

☆

Former Secretary of State Dean Rusk said there are three categories of age: youth, middle age, and "Gee, you're looking well."

☆

If there ever was a politician who proved that taking action was better than taking a poll it was Winston

Churchill. When a political rival said that it was time for leaders to keep their ears to the ground, Churchill replied, "All I can say is that the British nation will find it very hard to look up to leaders who are detected in that somewhat ungainly posture."

☆

When he was a U.S. senator, Lyndon Johnson had the following sign in a prominent place in his office: "You ain't learnin' nothin' when you're talkin'."

☆

Nixon once mused, "I have often said that the one thing worse for a politician than being wrong is being dull. But it is better to be dull than to be silly."

☆

Ronald Reagan believed in appearances: "I have learned that one of the most important rules in politics is poise—which means looking like an owl after you have behaved like a jackass."

☆

Don Regan, who served as Secretary of the Treasury and Chief of Staff in the Reagan administration, earned a reputation for arrogance. He might have survived longer in Washington had he been able to poke fun at himself more often, like he did when he said, "I'm not arrogant. I just believe there's no human problem that couldn't be solved—if people would simply do as I tell 'em."

☆

The legendary Sam Rayburn was Speaker of the House when I was first elected to Congress in 1960. I'm sure he didn't know I was there, given his statement: "Anyone can be elected once by accident. Beginning with the second term, it's worth paying attention."

☆

Walter Mondale and I didn't agree on many political topics, but he hit the nail on the head when he said, "If you are sure you understand everything that is going on, you are hopelessly confused."

☆

Elizabeth and I have long been admirers of Margaret Thatcher, and I wasn't about to argue with the "Iron Lady" when she said, "In politics, if you want anything said, ask a man; if you want anything done, ask a woman."

Partisanship

———— ☆ ————

L YNDON JOHNSON HAD a line I've
never forgotten. "I'd rather win a convert than
a fight," he said. Gerald Ford, himself a veteran of Capitol Hill, put it even better when he said
that in politics "there is no such thing as an enemy—
only someone who disagrees with you today and who
might be with you on the next vote."

Unfortunately, not everyone agrees with this
viewpoint. To some, consensus is a dirty word. Even
within my own party, I'm sorry to say, there are some
whose ideal Lincoln Day Dinner would probably fea-
ture John Wilkes Booth as an honored guest. I say
this as a former chairman of the Republican National
Committee, and as one who proudly defended Presidents Nixon, Ford, Reagan, and Bush against Democrat attacks.

But one should never confuse partisanship with
character assassination. As Republican National

Chairman during Watergate, I regularly rejected White House p.r. proposals that were supposed to drive a stake through Democrat hearts. Among the most offensive of these was a cartoon showing Senator George McGovern in a Vietcong uniform. In my acceptance speech at the 1996 Republican National Convention, I took my gloves off, and listed the many failings of the Clinton administration. But I also told my fellow Republicans that the President was "my opponent and not my enemy."

Is there a happy medium between political pablum and slander? I thought I found it on election night 1992. On learning that the voters had made me (no doubt quite unintentionally) the highest elected Republican official in the country, I extended congratulations to President-elect Clinton. At the same time, I couldn't resist seeing the outcome as a split decision. The good news, I said, was that Bill Clinton, like all Presidents, would be getting a Washington, D.C., honeymoon. The bad news was that I would be his chaperon.

☆ ☆ ☆

During a speech, Theodore Roosevelt took on a heckler who proclaimed, "I'm a Democrat!"

"May I ask the gentleman why he's a Democrat?" Roosevelt inquired.

"My grandfather was a Democrat, my father was a Democrat, and I'm a Democrat."

"My friend," Roosevelt asked, "suppose your grandfather had been a jackass and your father was a jackass, what would you be?"

"A Republican!"

☆

Teddy also said, "A gentleman told me recently he doubted if I would vote for the angel Gabriel if he was found at the head of the Democratic Party, to which I responded that the angel Gabriel would never be found in such company."

☆

Woodrow Wilson once said, "Now, I have long enjoyed the friendship and companionship of Republicans, because I am by instinct a teacher, and I would like to teach them something."

☆

The humorist Dorothy Parker had a scathing reaction when informed of ex-President Coolidge's death in January 1933. Said Parker, "How could they tell?"

☆

The symbol of Alf Landon's uphill campaign in 1936 was—what else?—the Kansas sunflower. FDR took some of the wind out of GOP sails by telling reporters, strictly off the record, that the sunflower was yellow, that it had a black heart, and that it was only good for feeding parrots. Roosevelt supporters went even further, flooding the country with bumper stickers that proclaimed, "Sunflowers Die in November."

☆

When Franklin Roosevelt ran for a third term in 1940, a Republican candidate for the Vermont legislature declared his support. A Vermont Republican challenged his colleague's divided party loyalty. "What are you," he asked the man, "a Republican or a Democrat? I want an honest answer."

"I'll give you an honest answer," replied the candidate. "I am a politician."

☆

Roosevelt liked to tell a story about meeting an old neighbor during his third-term campaign. "Who are you voting for this year?" Roosevelt asked.

The man replied, "For the Republicans."

"How come? Does the third term bother you?"

"Oh, it isn't that at all, Franklin," the neighbor replied. "It's just that, frankly, I voted Republican the first time you ran, I voted Republican the second time you ran, and I'm going to vote Republican again—because I never had it so good!"

☆

Truman remarked, "Republicans don't like people to talk about depressions. You remember the old saying, 'Don't talk about rope in the house of somebody who has to be hanged.'"

"Whenever a fellow tells me he's bipartisan," Truman noted, "I know he's going to vote against me."

☆

Truman also wondered why "when a leader is in the Democratic Party he's a boss; but when he's in the Republican Party he's a leader."

☆

I never knew longtime Kentucky senator and Truman administration Vice President Alben Barkley, but given his reputation for humor, I know I would have liked him. One of my favorite Barkleyisms is: "A bureaucrat is a Democrat who holds some office that a Republican wants."

☆

During his 1952 presidential campaign, Adlai Stevenson said, "I will make a bargain with the Republicans. If they stop telling lies about Democrats, we will stop telling the truth about them."

Stevenson on Republicans: "The elephant has a thick skin, a head full of ivory, and as everyone who has seen a circus parade knows, proceeds best by grasping the tail of his predecessor."

☆

Dwight Eisenhower on Democrats: "The Democratic Party is not one, but two political parties with the same name. They unite only once every two years—to wage political campaigns."

☆

After the 1964 Democratic landslide nearly destroyed the Republican Party, Lyndon Johnson surveyed the election results and said, "I think it's very important that we have a two-party system. I am a fellow that likes small parties, and the Republican Party is about the size I like."

At a fund-raising dinner for the Democratic Party in June 1964, Lyndon Johnson quipped, "This is not a partisan dinner. It is open to any member of any political party who wants to contribute one hundred dollars to the Democratic Party in November."

☆

After his nomination as vice presidential candidate, Hubert Humphrey was invited by Lyndon Johnson to spend a weekend at the LBJ ranch. During the visit, Johnson invited him for a parley in a cow pasture, where Humphrey promptly stepped in a pile of manure. "Mr. President," declared Humphrey as soon as he regained his equanimity, "I just stepped on the Republican platform!"

In April 1964, Humphrey arrived by plane at a campaign stop in Fargo, North Dakota. The event was thronged. He walked down the plane's ramp and told the crowd, "I couldn't believe my eyes when I saw this huge crowd so late at night. For a moment I felt like a Republican: I thought I was walking in my sleep."

☆

Following a prolonged illness in 1964, Senator Everett Dirksen returned to the Senate floor in a decidedly forensic frame of mind. Here is a sample of the kind of exquisitely articulate political wit and aplomb that virtually died with Dirksen: "We Republicans are very literal and, frequently, literate people. When we read perfectly plain English we are invariably led into taking it at face value. If we read that capital investment should be encouraged, that consumer purchasing power should be stimulated, that consumers should be protected, or, for example, that higher education should be encouraged, who can censure us—except possibly for our innocence—for believing that any proposals we might make to hasten these ends would not receive White House approval, even active support?

"So perhaps you can imagine my bedridden amazement, my pajama-fuffled consternation, yes, my pill-laden astonishment this week to learn that three Republican-sponsored proposals to assist in achieving these laudable goals had been defeated by very narrow margins, victims of that new White House telephonic half nelson known as the Texas Twist.

"To those of you on the Democratic side of the aisle who are still rubbing your bruised arms, I can only extend my sympathy and hope that you who must face the electorate this fall won't need it. To you on the Republican side of the aisle, I happily extend my admiration and gratitude for the unanimous support you gave each of the three proposals. When Republicans stand together, without a single defector, on three crucial Senate votes, then the entire nation must know we were right."

☆

One of Morris Udall's favorite stories was about an Arizona Democrat who lost a race for mayor of Tombstone. He told the victorious Republican:

"The election is now over.
Let all this bitterness pass.
I will hug your elephant and
You can kiss my . . . donkey."

☆

Eugene McCarthy noted, "In Minnesota, the Republicans are like the lowest form of existence. They don't have much life or vitality at the height of their existence, but they never die."

☆

As Ronald Reagan's Ambassador to the United Nations, Jeane Kirkpatrick earned a reputation as someone who called them like she saw them. She did just that when she said, "The Democrats are in a real bind. They won't get elected unless things get worse—and things won't get worse unless they're elected."

☆

During Reagan's first year in office, the Republican legislative program surged through Congress like a forty-ton tank. The Democrats practically had no choice but to go along with what amounted to the virtual dissolution of the last vestiges of the New Deal.

As Speaker of the House, Tip O'Neill was the most prominent Democrat caught in the onslaught. In his memoirs, he wrote that he felt "like the guy in the old joke who gets hit by a steamroller. Somebody runs to tell his wife about the accident.

" 'I'm taking a bath right now,' she says. 'Could you just slip him under the door?' "

☆

Speaking to Democrats in 1980, Reagan said, "I know what it's like to pull the Republican lever for the first time, because I used to be a Democrat myself, and I can tell you it only hurts for a minute and then it feels just great."

Reagan on Democrats: "The leaders of the Democratic Party have gone so far left, they've left the country."

In one of his last public appearances, President Reagan told the following story to a group of supporters at the Reagan Presidential Library in California. It seems there was a much-married woman who walked into a bridal shop one day and told the salesclerk that she was looking for a wedding gown for her *fourth* wedding.

"Well," replied the salesclerk, "exactly what type of dress are you looking for?"

"A long, frilly white dress with a veil."

The salesclerk didn't know quite what to say. "Frankly, madam, dresses of that nature are considered more appropriate for brides who are being married the first time—for those who are a bit more innocent, if you know what I mean."

"Well," replied the customer, more than a little put out, "I can assure you that I am as innocent as the rest of them. Believe it or not, despite all my marriages, I remain as innocent as any first-time bride.

"You see," she went on, "my first husband was a dear sweet man. Unfortunately, all the excitement of the wedding was simply too much for him and he died as we checked into the hotel on our wedding night."

"I'm so sorry to hear that," said the salesclerk. "But what about the others?"

"Well, my second husband and I got into a terrible fight in the limousine on the way to our wedding reception. We haven't spoken since and got the marriage annulled quickly."

"What about your third husband?" asked the salesclerk.

"Well," said the woman, "he was a Democrat. And every night for four years he just sat on the edge of the bed and told me how *good* it was going to be!"

☆

No one in recent memory has riled congressional Democrats more than Newt Gingrich. Gingrich predicted that "if I announced today I was buying vanilla ice cream for every child in America, [House

Democratic whip] David Bonior would jump up and say, 'He wants them all to have heart attacks.' "

☆

One great joke that's been around forever concerns the two newly elected Democrat congressmen who were discussing campaign tactics. One insisted that it was very important to gain the support of taxi drivers, because they spoke with hundreds of passengers each day. The congressman then detailed how he would engage in friendly conversations with cabdrivers, compliment their driving skills, and leave them a large tip. "Then just as they drive away," he concluded, "I stick my head in the window and say, 'Vote Democrat.' "

While admiring the technique, his Democrat colleague said he had used a more effective method. "Before I leave the cab," he said, "I toss a lighted match on the back seat, slash the tires, and spit on the window. Then I stick my head in on the driver's side and shout in his face, 'Vote Republican.' "

Liberal/Conservative

———————————— ☆ ————————————

IT'S UNFORTUNATE THAT in recent years the divergent strains of American political thought have been reduced to bumper-sticker simplicity. You know the caricatures: conservatives declaring, "Whatever it is, I'm against it"; liberals proclaiming, "Whatever it costs, I'm for it." More recently, the media has gotten into the act, pretending amazement that not every conservative agrees with every other conservative. I don't know about you, but with all due respect to Elizabeth, I can't think of two people, let alone two hundred million, who have identical views on every issue. I belong to a political party, not a cult.

Moreover, conservatism has undergone many changes since I went into politics. Even before first deciding to run for Congress in 1960, one of the first things I did was to render homage to a local power broker named Dane Hansen. A cornfed boss whose influence and connections made him pivotal in choosing any GOP nominee, Hansen was as unconventional in his personal habits as he was orthodox in his political outlook. He liked to start his workday around the supper hour, holding court with visiting politicians or businessmen in his home in northwestern Kansas, and rarely going to bed before dawn. It took me only one nocturnal visit to convince the kingmaker that I could be ideologically trusted. As I heard it later, Hansen told friends, "Hell, I knew Dole was a fiscal conservative. The tires on his car were threadbare."

Back then, it was fashionable for opinion makers to mock conservatives as a bunch of little old ladies from Pasadena who wore tennis shoes and reserved their greatest indignation for the evils of fluoridation. Conservatives, it was claimed, refused to look at a new moon out of respect for the old one. They didn't laugh so much as they were laughed at. Ronald Reagan changed all this, as he changed so much of Washington's conventional wisdom, simply by demonstrating that not every conservative Republican had embalming fluid in his veins.

I remember the time Ted Kennedy tried to make an issue out of Reagan's age. Attending a ninetieth birthday party for Averell Harriman, Teddy declared Reagan's ideas to be twice as old as the guest of honor. Rising to the challenge, President

Reagan acknowledged that his ideas were, in fact, nearly two hundred years old. Most of them could be found in the Constitution, which had been drawn up to place limitations on government's exercise of power.

Ted Kennedy is unabashedly and proudly a liberal. In fact, I often joked that one day on the Senate floor when discussing a long-ago debate, I said, "Gentlemen, let me tax your memories on this topic." Teddy then jumped up and said, "Why haven't I thought of that before?"

Despite our political and philosophical differences, I'm proud to call Ted a friend. His mother, Rose, celebrated her birthday on July 22, as did I. And on the first July 22 after her death, I sent Ted a note saying that my thoughts and prayers were with him. He replied with a gracious note saying that if his mother were alive, she would wish me luck in a run for the presidency—but not too much luck.

★ ★ ★

"Conservatism is the policy of making no change and consulting your grandmother when in doubt."

—WOODROW WILSON

☆

"A conservative man is a man who just sits and thinks, mostly sits."

— WOODROW WILSON

☆

Famed for his frugality, Calvin Coolidge halted the twenty-one-gun salutes customarily fired as the presidential yacht *Mayflower* drew up alongside George Washington's Mount Vernon. They made his white collie, Prudence Prim, howl. Besides, explained Coolidge, "it costs money to fire so many guns. So I have the band play 'The Star-Spangled Banner' instead."

☆

Dwight Eisenhower remarked, "The middle of the road is all of the usable surface. The extremes, right and left, are in the gutters."

☆

"Do you know the difference between cannibals and liberals?" asked a frustrated Lyndon Johnson in 1967. "Cannibals eat only their enemies."

☆

In his autobiography, Ronald Reagan remembered his days as a "hemophilic liberal": "I have come to realize that a great many so-called liberals aren't liberal—they will defend to the death your right to agree with them."

Defining Communists, Reagan said, "Well, it's someone who reads Marx and Lenin." And how do you tell an anti-Communist? "It's someone who understands Marx and Lenin."

Differences that arose among his many aides made Reagan admit, "Sometimes our right hand doesn't know what our far-right hand is doing."

☆

Tough-talking Frank Rizzo, the late mayor of Philadelphia, once bluntly proclaimed, "A liberal is a conservative who hasn't been mugged yet."

☆

Robert Frost described a liberal as someone "who won't take his own side in a quarrel."

Retirement

─────── ✩ ───────

DEMOCRACY, NEEDLESS TO SAY, is a fickle employer, but even when the voters terminate your contract, that's no reason—or excuse—to lick your wounds or indulge in self-pity. Consider America's former Presidents, for instance. They may be out of office but they are hardly retired, as President Ford noted at the 1997 rededication of his Presidential Museum in Grand Rapids, Michigan. Sharing the platform with two other members of the world's most exclusive trade union, Ford paid tribute to Jimmy Carter's humanitarian works, so numerous and far-flung that at times it seems as if Carter must live on an airplane.

President Bush, on the other hand, prefers to jump out of planes. According to Ford, the forty-first President had even invited the thirty-eighth President to accompany him on his highly publicized parachute mission.

"Not gonna do it," replied Ford, mimicking Dana Carvey's distinctive Bushspeak. "Wouldn't be prudent." Besides, added Ford, "after all those jokes about my golf swing, do you really want to tempt fate by having me jump out of a plane?"

I took a leap of my own in 1997, joining the Washington, D.C., law firm Verner, Lipfert, where I found myself in the company of such prominent Democrats as former senator George Mitchell and former Texas governor Ann Richards. These days I bring my dog to work, just in case I need a Republican to talk to.

Naturally, it's great to be working with my old Senate colleague from Maine, who found it easier to fix Northern Ireland than the United States Senate. Some days we gridlock the entire law firm for old times' sake. I may be new, but I'm quickly learning the ways of the successful Washington lawyer. At an early party, I thanked everyone for taking fifteen minutes out of their crowded schedule to welcome me to the firm—or, as I've since learned to call it, two billable hours.

To make my "retirement" a little more exciting, in the early months of 1998, when Monica Lewinsky became a media preoccupation, I was in the rather embarrassing position of being Lewinsky's next-door neighbor at the Watergate. The *New York Times* asked me if I had seen my famous neighbor. I acknowledged that I had. "I walk by fast," I reassured the *Times.* "I don't want to be subpoenaed!"

☆ ☆ ☆

William Howard Taft tipped the presidential scales at 350-plus pounds. On leaving the White House, Yale, his alma mater, offered him a Chair of Law. Given his size, said Taft, a Sofa of Law would be more appropriate.

Not long after his defeat in the 1912 presidential election, William Howard Taft delivered a wry valedictory before New York's Lotos Club. His theme: what are we to do with our former Presidents? With his tongue firmly in cheek, Taft proposed "a dose of chloroform or . . . the fruit of the Lotos tree" as a means to protect his countrymen "from the troublesome fear that the occupant [of the nation's highest office] could ever come back." As for the suggestion from William Jennings Bryan that all former Presidents become ex officio members of the Senate, Taft was dubious. "If I must go and disappear into oblivion," he chuckled, "I prefer to go by the chloroform method. It's pleasanter and less drawn out."

☆

In 1930 former President Calvin Coolidge filled out a membership form for the Washington Press Club. At the place marked "Occupation," he wrote in "Retired." Then he skipped down a line to the section marked "Comments." Coolidge thought for a moment before writing "And glad of it."

A reluctant Coolidge was lured out of his retirement to deliver a major campaign address for Herbert Hoover at Madison Square Garden in October 1932. After he was through, a woman rushed up and exclaimed, "Oh, Mr. Coolidge, what a wonderful address. I stood up all through it."

"So did I," said Coolidge.

☆

When he was asked what retired Presidents did, Herbert Hoover replied, "We spend our time taking pills and dedicating libraries."

Not long before he died, Hoover was asked how he had managed to survive the wilderness years that began in 1933 and ended only with the death of his onetime friend and later bitter antagonist, Franklin D. Roosevelt. "It was simple," said Hoover. "I outlived the bastards."

☆

When Dean Acheson resigned as Secretary of State at the beginning of the Eisenhower administration in 1952, he said, "I will undoubtedly have to seek what is happily known as gainful employment, which I am glad to say does not describe holding public office."

☆

Once out of office, Harry Truman observed that there are three things which can ruin a man—"money, power, and women. I never had any money, I never wanted power, and the only woman in my life is up at the house right now."

☆

Shortly after leaving the White House, Truman commented that he had received over 70,000 letters since the end of his presidency. "All except a hundred of those were favorable," said the President, "and those few, of course, were from friends."

☆

In the late 1950s, a reporter asked Churchill whether he had any plans to retire. He replied, "Not until I am a great deal worse and the Empire a great deal better."

Told that a fellow Londoner in his late seventies had been arrested in Hyde Park for making improper advances toward a young girl in the dead of winter, Winston Churchill quipped, "Over seventy-five and below zero! Makes you *proud* to be an Englishman!"

Late Night

⎯⎯⎯⎯ ☆ ⎯⎯⎯⎯

S INCE I BEGAN this book by writing about my November 1996 appearance on *The Late Show with David Letterman*, it's only fitting that I close with a few "zingers" from Letterman and his late-night competitor Jay Leno. One thing Letterman and Leno have taught me is the truth of the old saying that "if you dish it out, you have to be able to take it." Throughout the 1996 campaign, Dave and Jay delighted night after night at poking fun at (among other things) my age, my crankiness, and my speaking ability. I was often asked if I objected to being the subject of the late-night monologues. The best response comes from Elizabeth, who was asked that same question by Jay Leno during an appearance on his show. "Not if you don't mind being audited by the IRS after Bob is elected," she quipped.

Here are some of Jay and Dave's "best."

☆ ☆ ☆

JAY LENO

"In a stunning admission on *Larry King Live* last night, Bob Dole revealed he is one of the test subjects for Viagra. He said on Larry King, 'I wish I had bought stock in it.' Only a Republican would think the best part of Viagra is the fact that you could make money off of it."

"Bob Dole is so old he got Grecian Formula from the original Grecian."

Leno on reports that there might be life on Mars: "Even wilder things came in today. Now they claim to have found life in the Dole campaign."

Leno on Dole campaign fever sweeping the country: "I haven't seen excitement like this since that time we almost switched to the metric system."

"You know what the hot drink going around L.A. is? The cool new drink? These Metamucil cocktails. Who drinks orange Metamucil shooters? I mean, besides Bob Dole on spring break?"

Leno, on Senator Strom Thurmond and me campaigning in South Carolina: "When Bob Dole stands next to Strom Thurmond, he looks like the new lifeguard on *Baywatch*."

☆ ☆ ☆

DAVID LETTERMAN

"Of the candidates currently running for President, most lived through Vietnam and the Cold War. A few even lived through the Second World War and the Great Depression. But only one candidate lived through the Civil War, the Declaration of Independence, and Columbus's Discovery of the New World. Elect Bob Dole. He's one thousand years old."

"Bob Dole thinks Hartford's a great place to hold a presidential debate because it's the life insurance capital of the world. Dole is so old his insurance agent is John Hancock."

As I got ready to go to San Diego to accept my party's nomination for President, Dave came up with a list of the top ten ways I was preparing for the Convention. My favorites on the list: "Agonizing over whether he'll support statehood for Michigan"; "Standing in front of the mirror, working on his 'acceptance scowl'"; and "Supervising the inflation of ten thousand balloons by Dan Quayle."

Of my complaints that campaigning is more difficult today, Dave quipped: "When Bob Dole first ran for office, of course it was easier. There were only thirteen colonies then."

Of one of my campaign trips to California: "He had lunch at McDonald's; coincidentally they've named a new sandwich after Bob Dole—it's the Arch Conservative."

Don't feel too bad for me. The appearance of this book coincides with the fiftieth anniversary of Harry Truman's stunning upset of Tom Dewey in 1948, which not only changed the course of American history but produced a patron saint for every political underdog since. Like Truman, I have a Midwestern preference for plain speaking, and a sometimes impolitic habit of laughing at pomposity. Although there have been times when I've been forced to eat my words—or swallow my pride—I still find it hard to take too seriously people who take themselves that way.

What people often forget is that the last laugh doesn't belong to the victorious candidate—it belongs to the late-night comics.

Afterword

―――――――― ☆ ――――――――

☆ ☆ ☆

CAMPAIGN 2000

OR SOME REASON, campaigns seem a lot funnier when you are not one of the candidates. And the 2000 race for the White House has already provided me—and other observers of the political scene—with plenty of opportunities for laughter. Indeed, I am serving as a Campaign 2000 commentator on *The Daily Show*, hosted by Jon Stewart on the Comedy Central network.

Even though I'm not on the 2000 ballot, a few barbs were still directed at me when, in 1999, Elizabeth spent a number of months exploring the possibility of entering the presidential race. Pundits delighted in speculating if I would enjoy certain traditional duties like selecting china and hosting state dinners. My standard response was that it sounded like a great job to me. I would have all the perks that come with the presidency—a car, a driver, Air Force One, the White House—and none of the responsibilities. Besides, I'd be making history. I pointed out in 1996 that America had never had a President named Bob.

I was very proud of Elizabeth's exploratory efforts in 1999. Wherever she traveled, she attracted huge crowds, many of whom had never before been involved in the political process. She also managed to keep her sense of humor intact. She brought down the house at a large New York City gathering when she explained, "Some pundits say that I'm too scripted, but my notes tell me that isn't so."

Once Elizabeth decided to close down her exploratory committee because of a fund-raising disadvantage, I quickly turned my attention to the other Campaign 2000 candidates to see how they were dealing with the late-night jokes. As I watched the programs, I smiled with the thought that it was better them than me.

Current Senate Majority Leader Trent Lott is to be commended for his vision in beginning the "Leader's Lecture" series. This is a speaking series where former Majority Leaders or Presidents of the Senate have been invited to reflect upon their careers before the Senate and invited guests in the historic Old Senate Chamber. On March 28, 2000, I had the honor of being the sixth speaker in the series.

While most of my speech would have been considered serious as I recounted ten especially memorable days out of the ten thousand or so I served in the Senate, I also made it a point to comment on humor and its necessary role in Congress and in life. During my remarks, I observed, "I also happen to believe that it is easier to get things done in this place with a sense of humor. After all, the United States is probably the only country on Earth that puts the pursuit of happiness right after life and liberty among our God-given rights. Laughter and liberty go well together. Indeed, as a weapon against injustice, ridicule can be as effective as moral outrage. I tried 'outrage' in 1996."

Consider the irrepressible Barry Goldwater. On being blackballed by an anti-Semitic country club in Phoenix, Goldwater responded, "Since I'm only half Jewish, can I join if I only play nine holes?"

Comedians—and other candidates—have taken advantage of the Vice President's occasional habit of exaggerating his own accomplishments. When, after both candidates clinched their party's nominations in March, Gore e-mailed a campaign challenge to Governor Bush, the Governor quickly e-mailed back that "this Internet thing you invented is neat." Now, Gore can't find the e-mail.

Governor Bush inherited a quick wit from his mother.

In fact, not only is Mrs. Bush funny, but she has a quick and self-deprecating style that endears her to all. A recent example is that after leaving the White House, Mrs. Bush joked that she never understood the so-called "fashion mavens" who criticized her wardrobe. "The fact is," she laughed, "My clothes are great, it's me that doesn't look so good."

As usual, however, it is the late-night comedians who are mining the most laughs from this campaign. Here are a number of their "zingers," and the political targets they "zinged."

★ ★ ★

JAY LENO

"Vice President Gore has announced that he will make campaign finance reform the cornerstone of his campaign. And he also announced that for $10,000 you can have your name inscribed on that corner-stone."

"It is so cold in New Hampshire today, Steve Forbes' tongue got stuck to the silver spoon in his mouth. In fact, they had to jump start Al Gore it was so cold."

"You know, I was watching the State of the Union last night and the President speaking at the Capitol. Did you notice behind him an oil painting? I'm wondering, Whose portrait is that? It looks familiar. And then I realize it's not an oil painting, it was Al Gore!"

On Groundhog Day: "Wasn't it nice to finally see something crawling out of a hole in the ground that wasn't running for President?"

"In 1996, Steve Forbes got 12 percent of the vote in New Hampshire and he spent $30 million; this year he got 13 percent . . . so at this rate in 150 years he could go back and win this thing!"

"You hear about this? Earlier today computer hackers actually shut down Al Gore for two hours."

"Steve Forbes has officially dropped out of the presidential race. He said he wanted to spend more time with his servants."

"Do you do this with Christmas lights? You have a string of them and one bulb is dead, and you flick the bulb with your finger to get it to light up? Same thing they do with George W. Bush before a debate."

☆ ☆ ☆

DAVID LETTERMAN

"Here's good news, though. The folks who make Sudafed, in a couple of weeks are going to introduce a brand-new, non-drowsy Al Gore."

"I don't know how you can be in politics and just not get sick and tired of yourself."

On the failed Mars Polar Lander: "This thing has been quieter than George W. Bush after a foreign policy question."

"I've got a big night planned. I'm going to take mom to see the movie *The Legend of Sleepy Hollow.* Y'know, you think about it, 'Sleepy Hollow' are two words that describe Al Gore. Sleepy. Hollow."

On political books. "It's hard not to be cynical about this new political memoir, *Growing up Jewish* by Hillary Clinton."

"Big news from outer space: astronomers have located a solar system 153 light-years away from earth.

That's the same distance Al Gore is trying to generate between himself and President Clinton."

☆ ☆ ☆

CONAN O'BRIEN

On the Iowa caucuses: "Senator Orrin Hatch announced that he is going to drop out of the presidential race this week. But first, Hatch has to tell everyone he was in the presidential race."

"Due to a problem that they were having yesterday with Air Force Two, Al Gore had to take a US Airways shuttle back to Washington. Reportedly, Gore spent the entire flight in the full upright and locked position."

"Hotel guests at the New York Sheraton were surprised when Al Gore came into the hotel's gym and ran on the treadmill. Guests said the main reason they were surprised is they didn't know Gore's legs moved."

☆ ☆ ☆

JON STEWART

"Elizabeth Dole endorsed Bush, Kennedy taps Gore, Gary Bauer preapproved for a Discover Card . . . Despite Liddy's endorsement, Republican opponent John McCain was not bitter, and said that he and the Doles remain the closest of friends, and he plans to have them over to the house for a little light conversation . . . perhaps about the seven years he spent in a bamboo box, squishing cockroaches into a protein mash, all for a little something called America."

"The gloves came off in last night's Republican debate. A political event so significant it literally leaps out at you from page twenty-three of today's *New York Times*."

☆ ☆ ☆

BILL MAHER

"It's a big week for endorsements, because I guess now that we're, like, weeks away from deciding this whole election . . . Liddy Dole yesterday for Bush, today Ted Kennedy for Al Gore. And Pat Buchanan said he's expecting a big upsurge now, because with the Y2K thing behind us, his constituents are now free to leave thier bunkers."

★ ★ ★

CRAIG KILBORN

"Forbes said he doesn't know yet whether he will run again for President or just fly his Lear jet over a forest fire and toss $60 million out the window."

"Elizabeth Dole has officially endorsed George W. Bush for the Republican presidential nomination . . . George W. Bush said he was especially pleased by Dole's endorsement because it showed that the pineapple industry is solidly behind him."

★

The picking was so ripe during the 2000 campaign that even reporters couldn't help but take a shot or two.

★ ★ ★

TOM BROKAW

"Al Gore seems to be like those kids who believe everything their parents write about them in the Christmas letter."

★ ★ ★

CHRIS MATTHEWS

"What's the story on Steve Forbes? Has he got that schizoid thing where the body doesn't move? He's like a 'Riverdancer.' Nothing moves above the waist!"

★

Maybe with regard to the political campaign season and television pundits, former Democratic nominee Michael Dukakis has it right. When asked if he had watched the "debate" on *Meet the Press* between Gore and Bradley, he answered, "I don't watch those Sunday shows. I was painting a room on my third floor."

☆

As we close out the 2000 campaign, it's no secret which of the two candidates has my support. But I would offer the same advice to whichever of the two happens to fall a few votes short come Election Day: Do what I did. Get yourself on a late-night show two days after the election, and keep laughing.

———————— ✪ ————————

B O B   D O L E is recognized as one of the nation's most prominent political figures of the twentieth century. Known for his effectiveness as a consensus builder in his thirty-five years in Congress, Senator Dole was the longest-serving Republican Leader in Senate history. He was also Chairman of the Republican National Committee, the 1976 Republican nominee for Vice-President, and the 1996 Republican nominee for President. He currently is serving as the Chairman of the World War II Memorial campaign and as Chairman of the International Commission on Missing Persons in Bosnia. Wounded in World War II, Senator Dole was awarded two Purple Hearts and a Bronze Star. He is married to Elizabeth Hanford Dole, former President of the American Red Cross, and lives in Washington, D.C.